How To Listen–
How To Be Heard

How To Listen—
How To Be Heard

Thomas G. Banville

Nelson-Hall/Chicago

Library of Congress Cataloging in Publication Data

Banville, Thomas G
    How to listen—how to be heard.

    Includes bibliographical references and index.
    1. Listening.   I. Title.
BF323.L5B3   153   77-17961
ISBN 0–88229–332–X (*cloth*)
ISBN 0–88229–559–4 (*paper*)

Copyright © 1978 by Thomas G. Banville

Manufactured in the United States of America

I don't take your words
Merely as words.
Far from it.

I listen
To what makes you talk—
Whatever that is—
And me listen.

Shinkichi Takahashi
After Images

Contents

Preface

There are many people to whom I am indebted in producing this book. The late Dr. C. Edson Caldwell was a teacher and good friend who inspired me at the beginning of my career in psychology. Professors James A. Saum and Robert A. Good of the California State University at Sacramento have entered and enriched my life at crucial times, perhaps without even knowing how much they meant to me.

Several of my colleagues have contributed encouragement and ideas. William R. Leek is an educational psychologist and a good friend with whom I have worked closely and exchanged therapy for the past several years. Doral F. Leek, a clinical psychologist, provided a quote which became the germ of the book, and he has added to it from his understated wisdom during many pleasant lunches.

Added inspiration came from many of the people listed in my chapter notes. I was especially impressed by the Gestalt Therapy of the late Frederick S. Perls. Carl Rogers has influenced my beliefs in regard to psychology and counseling for more than twenty-five years.

Certain parts of chapters 5, 7, and 13 have appeared in *Early Years*, © Allen Raymond, Inc., and in *Family Digest*, © Our Sunday Visitor. The author is grateful to these publishers for permission to reprint this material.

One person more than any other helped make it possible for me to write this book. Because of her patience when I was unavailable as a companion, because of her constructive and honest criticism when I missed the mark completely, because of her assistance as a typist—and most of all because of her unwavering belief in the project and in me, I dedicate this work to Margaret, my wife.

Introduction

Let me state at the outset that my reason for wanting to write this book was not that I considered myself a good listener and you a poor one. It was, on the contrary, my realization that I was not as good a listener as I should be which prompted me to seek ways of improving my skills. In these pages I merely share with you the ways I have found.

The title of this book suggests that there may be something amiss with the way you listen. That's very likely true. Most of us—even many of us in the so-called "helping" professions—listen very poorly. One study, for example, disclosed that school counselors didn't listen as well as the teachers who sent students to them.

In the pages that follow you will find a key to more effective listening. That's the main thrust of this work. But more than that you will discover how to be more effective in your interpersonal relationships. If you're a parent, you will learn how to foster good listening habits in your children.

Some of the difficulty we have in listening and relating to others is due to the fact that we tend to limit the number of feelings we permit ourselves to experience. Most often the limitation is an unconscious one and concerns who and what we perceive ourselves to be—our ego or self-structure.

Self-structure is a tremendously important factor in listening. It not only serves as an anchor point in one's daily interactions with the environment, but it's also essential in directing one's behavior. Built into your self-structure are certain assumptions by which you live.

These assumptions fall into three categories. First is your assumption of what is real—your view of how things really are, what you're really like, and what the world is really like. The second assumption concerns your value system—what's good or bad, right or wrong, how things should be and the kinds of polarization which govern your behavior.

Through the medium of this book you will explore the first two assumptions and become as aware as possible of how they limit your ability to feel. You will use that awareness to start expanding your store of feelings. Next you will learn how to express your own feelings clearly and how to control them so that they help your ability to communicate rather than interfere with it. Then you will see how to overcome the effects of the inner conflicts which are the natural consequences of the first two assumptions.

Finally you will use your ability to recognize and express your own feelings creatively, to help you identify the feelings of others, and to respond to them in a way which will enhance mutual and self-understanding. The process by which you will develop these skills will, at appropriate points, involve you actively. This is not merely a theoretical presentation, although necessary theoretical background is provided. It's a practical guide.

Assumption number three involves your idea of how things could be and of your possibilities for personal growth. It's assumption number three that motivated you to pick up this book. One final word before you get into the meat of it: That word is "practice."

Remember that this book can provide only a beginning. The extent to which you daily use the techniques and principles set forth will determine the amount of personal growth you enjoy. This is not a book to be read and put on the shelf to gather dust. The points presented may appear simple, but that is deceptive. You will need to make frequent reference to them.

Part I

Schizophrenic Listening: The Problem

1

What Do You Mean, Schizophrenic Listening?

Since this book is about listening, it will begin by making a case for listening. This seems necessary because listening is a skill which in my opinion is not accorded the lofty position in our culture which it deserves.

It has been said that no nation has ever become famous for its readers. That may be true, but without readers a nation's writers would also be unknowns. The analogy could be made that no nation ever became famous for its listeners, but without them . . . well, as philosophers ask, "What is the sound of one hand clapping? And if a tree falls in the forest, does it make any sound if no one is there to hear it?"

A bumper sticker I've seen on several automobiles reads "Sex is the nicest thing two people can do for each other." I take exception to that claim—not, certainly, because I'm opposed to sex. I agree with another sticker on the same subject which claims that "Sex is the most fun you can have without laughing." But I would accord the art of listening a status above that of sex if I were to rank-

3

order the two in a list of nice things we can do for each other.

The need to be heard is so great that if being listened to were completely absent from one's daily existence, one would probably begin talking to oneself. Man needs feedback of all kinds from his environment, and among the most satisfying kinds of feedback is the knowledge that one is being listened to when one wishes to be heard.

Defoe recognized this need when he wrote *Robinson Crusoe*; so did Dumas in *The Count of Monte Cristo*. The ghost of Hamlet's father could not rest until he was heard by his son, and God populated the Garden of Eden with two people, assuming perhaps mistakenly that they would listen to one another. Some forms of mental illness appear to result from feeling that nobody is "out there" paying attention. Even infantile autism may be due to an absence of feedback from significant humans—parents, for example.

James and Jongeward state that "Listening is one of the finest strokes one person can give another."[1] The word "strokes" refers to the context of Dr. Thomas A. Harris' application of Eric Berne's *Transactional Analysis*. A positive stroke refers to any medium through which one person lets another know "You're O.K." Negative strokes tell the other person "You're not O.K."[2] There are times when a negative stroke is better than no stroke at all. One of those times is when the negative stroke comes in response to a statement. It indicates, at least, that the speaker was heard.

Listening, then, is not only an important part of human interaction; it's a vital one. And yet it seems characteristic of our communication pattern that everyone talks and nobody listens. But even if by some miracle everyone suddenly began listening one's fair share, the quality of that listening is still to be considered, and enormous differences in listening quality exist. Let's look first at some kinds of listening which are really nonlistening, and that will lead us into a description of schizophrenic listening.

In everyday existence one probably encounters many more expert talkers than skilled listeners. An interesting facet of that observation is that even among those whom one supposes to be good listeners, many are not really listening at all—but the speaker is oblivious to that because they pursue their nonlistening behavior actively. According to the following, albeit questionable source, the French excel in nonlistening.

A friend who spent some time attending school in France told me that Paris had a paucity of psychiatrists. I rushed off to Europe to check that out, and I can confirm his statement. At last count, in fact, only four psychiatrists carry on private practice in Paris.

Intrigued, my friend weighed a number of hypotheses which might account for the shortage. His first thesis was that Parisians simply didn't develop psychiatric problems. But in a large modern metropolis with its inherent stresses that hardly seemed likely. Or perhaps the large amounts of wine consumed by the French dulled their susceptibility to psychic stress or somehow served as a substitute for psychiatric help. My informant finally concluded that alcoholic consumption, though not the wine per se, did have some bearing on the matter. It was the environment in which the wine was consumed that served as the medium for catharsis. According to his theory the Parisians may have perfected a system widely used in our own country as well. When the stresses of life bear too heavily on them, they, as do millions of Americans, seek out the solace of the corner bar, or in their case the bistro. But there's one important difference.

Americans who frequent the corner bars unload their problems on the friendly bartender, whose psychiatric practice is easily as large as, although less financially rewarding than, that of most licensed practitioners. Parisians on the other hand generally speak to the bartender only when placing their orders. The remainder of talk is directed toward the person—friend or stranger—who occupies an adjacent stool. The person perched on that stool, however, is simultaneously talking at a neighboring stool-percher, and so on. The process is reminiscent of the family in Chekhov's play, *The Cherry Orchard*, whose only activity as a group was to talk past one another. In spite of this my friend insisted that therapy somehow was occurring, and that if all the bars in Paris were placed end-to-end, they would constitute the world's largest analyst's couch.

Now that is nonlistening *par excellence*, but it is not schizophrenic listening. I would place the Parisians' non-listening behavior much higher on the scale of ways in which one can ignore the speech of another. For one thing it would probably be safe to assume that the Parisians don't expect to be heard. The truth may be that they don't *want* to be heard, and that if they suspected for a moment that anyone were really listening, they would choose not to divulge their thoughts and feelings.

A kind of audition that's a bit lower on the acceptable listening scale is typified by a ready-to-retire psychiatrist whose office shared the same floor with that of another psychiatrist who had only recently entered practice. As they rode down on the elevator together at the end of each day, the younger man was astounded to see how fresh the older one appeared. Finally one day he decided to ask about it.

"You know," he said, "I'm continually amazed at how unfatigued you are at the end of the day. I mean no offense, but I'm obviously a much younger man. And yet after listening to patient after patient all day, I'm bushed. How do you do it?"

With a wry smile wrinkling his face the senior psychiatrist replied, "Who listens?"

That story comes a bit closer to illustrating schizophrenic listening. At least it demonstrates a situation in which the speaker—who in this case would be the psychiatrist's patient—expects to be heard during his fifty-minute hour. That doesn't necessarily mean that he wants to be heard, though—any more than the Parisian wants, if my guess is correct, to be heard by his fellow bistro patron.

I think the institutional setting has become an important factor. Sometimes the mere act of seeing a therapist in his office has an effect. It may not be the effect the therapist assumes, but it may be the effect the patient desires, the one he wanted all along—not to confide all, but rather to go through the motions of doing so under conditions socially established as therapeutic. Other formats exist in which the same kind of result may be obtained.

As a Roman Catholic I have always felt that in the confessional, too—even though the process itself is the primary thing—the institutional setting has come to predominate. I can recall, for example, a number of occasions when I had done something I'd just as soon the father confessor did not know about and I resorted to the "muffled speech ploy." And despite the supposed anonymity afforded by that darkened and curtained cubicle, I was certain that the priest, even if I had never been anywhere near his church before, knew exactly who I was. Nevertheless I sincerely believed, having been conditioned to do so, that going through the prescribed ritual would by itself remove whatever guilt I had accumulated for my misdeeds—and so it did. It seems to me in retrospect that the priest was more concerned with the institution than with the process of confession. He would probe what I had done (or neglected to do), my greater and lesser transgressions, my mortal and venial sins, and would somehow equate their total with a certain number of prayers of retribution. I seemed to have the knack, somehow always, to come up with culpabilities which rated "one Act of Contrition, five Our Fathers, and ten Hail Marys." It has been said that the one indispensable person in the confessional is the listener. But I would place the majority of priests who heard my confessions somewhere on the listening scale between a Parisian stool-percher and that elder psychiatrist.

In addition to being conditioned through religion to believe that confession will gain forgiveness, I am also conditioned through my professional training to believe that self-disclosure is necessary for the good of the soul. Perhaps I should just accept those beliefs as good and sufficient. But just once in the confessional I would like to have been asked how I *felt* about the sins I had committed. That would have given me a sign that I was actually being heard; and I think I would have welcomed it, even though perhaps I really didn't want to be heard. Nevertheless I would guess that no more nor less listening goes on in a confessional than is supposed to—and so a major characteristic of the schizophrenic listening process is still lacking: the earnest unfulfilled wish of the speaker to be heard by a person he believes is truly interested in what he wants to communicate.

Another kind of listening is extremely annoying, and I wager that you've experienced it, too. It's terribly frustrating to try telling something to another person when he or she interrupts to address someone else. This kind of thing is one major reason I detest cocktail parties. Just before the interruption you were answering a question about your line of work. After having turned to greet a newcomer, the social butterfly to whom you were just introduced then turns back and inquires, "Now what were you saying about Barry?" That's getting pretty close to schizophrenic listening because since you were asked a question you probably expected to be heard. But here too an important ingredient is lacking. In order for schizophrenic listening to happen, there must be a degree of emotional urgency on the part of the speaker. At the cocktail party one probably couldn't care less about giving details of one's employment than the other really cares about receiving them. Both are going through the ritualistic process of the cocktail circuit, and each will leave the encounter thinking he has made a new acquaintance.

Perhaps even more infuriating than that kind of inattentive listening is the technique of the Voice Raiser, who controls the conversation by literally outshouting everybody else. This person generally combines voice raising with a seemingly endless monologue which is kept flowing uninterruptedly. Despite the deftness of one's efforts to convert it to a dialogue, they're only defeated by increase in volume and pitch from the Voice Raiser. One doesn't expect to be listened to by the Voice Raiser because it's impossible even to be heard. And it's that fact, as we have seen—that one doesn't expect to be heard—which distinguishes the Voice Raiser, too, from the schizophrenic listening pattern.

These illustrations present some types of nonlistening which exemplify certain conditions. First, the speaker expects to be heard; and secondly, the speaker wants, at least on the face of it, to be heard. But in order for schizophrenic listening to happen, other conditions must also apply.

With these few examples of nonlistening as a background (and I'm sure you could give others), let's turn to an examination of what schizophrenic listening is and how listening affects relationships.

When students of communication look at the construction of conversation or "messages," one dichotomy which stands out under their collective magnifying glass is generally labeled "content vs. feeling." The content of the message is contained in the words uttered by the speaker and heard by the listener. The feeling, however, is contained not in the words spoken, but in the speaker on the one hand, in the listener on the other, and in what passes between them. Thus both elements are mutual transactions. Schizophrenic listening can result when, as frequently happens, the content of the message is not congruent with the speaker's feeling.

One of my colleagues with a fondness for examples of the obfuscatory use of language has the following quotation in his collection which illustrates the above point: "I know

that you believe you understand what you think I said,
but I am not at all sure you realize that what you heard
is not what I meant." There's so much truth in that statement for our present purposes that it's almost not funny.
I can't think of a more concise expression of the premise
of this book.

In what man has assumed to be his unique talent—
speech—many inherent difficulties exist which produce
unclear and contradictory messages. The semantic differ-
ential, for example, has been the subject of much study by
language specialists. We know that the emotional impact
of particular words and phrases varies from person to person and from group to group.

But just as important a factor in message confusion
is the matter of incongruence between content and feeling
just referred to. That confusion is partly the cause of what
I have labeled "schizophrenic listening." The incongruence
starts within the speaker. But in the matter of feeling
there is a further, more complex external incongruence
which can (and usually does) arise between speaker and
listener. The reason for that incongruence is found in the
differing views of the two about what constitutes reality
in the circumstances where message exchanges take place.

For example, because of a number of genealogical and
environmental factors which impinge upon our development, each of us focuses messages through a unique dis-
torting lens which is our own reality. By distorted, I mean
that because of factors we'll examine later one's own reality is not immediately available or clear to another. Indeed, without use of the special techniques this book will
provide, they may never be clear and available.

S. I. Hayakawa speaks of the "intensionally oriented"
and the "extensionally oriented" person. If one is intensionally oriented, one's preoccupation with words alone
causes, among other things, an unawareness of contexts.
The extensionally oriented person, on the other hand, is
governed not by words alone, but by the facts to which the

words lead.[3] Hayakawa says, "The meanings of words are not in the words, they are in us."[4] That is to say, if one listens to the words alone and not to the entire content of the speaker's message, one cannot understand the message because one hasn't sought its meaning. The meaning lies in the feelings of speaker and listener, not in the words.

Thus, returning to the term "schizophrenic listening," I intend the word "schizophrenic" to apply not directly to the listener alone, but to the dynamics involved between speaker and listener. We will see in the next chapter that the schizophrenic's speech can be unintelligible because his thought process is distorted by his reality and by associations which he apparently cannot make clear to his listener. Thus distorted, the schizophrenic listener makes his own associations from the speaker's words. This makes the meaning of the speaker's intended message unintelligible to him.

Among "normals" a sharing of realities is seldom fully accomplished, to be sure, but it is nevertheless distinctly possible. Acceptance of that idea is a basis for psychotherapeutic practice. Sharing takes place in the process of communication only when the listener's role is as active as the speaker's. For example, I as a listener to your message have an obligation to attempt, at least, to identify your reality and the affect, or feeling, that your message is intended to relate—not merely what your words mean, but what *you* mean. When I succeed in doing that, I can then help you to communicate and, perhaps more important, help you clarify your own feelings underlying your message.

But there is a presupposition here. Unless you are willing to share your feelings and your reality with me, you can force me to listen schizophrenically. Martin Buber once discussed his philosophy with Carl Rogers, the American psychologist. Buber, an existentialist, asked at one point whether Rogers' therapy works the same with schizophrenics as it does with normals. Elaborating on his question, Buber explained, "I can talk to a schizophrenic as far as he is willing to let me into his particular world that is his own . . . in general he does not want to have me come in."[5]

That seems to me precisely the point. If, as Buber puts it, it is a matter of the schizophrenic or anyone *willing* or *not willing* others to come into his life, there is the task. Schizophrenic listening means a not-willing of one's self to enter the other's particular world, or a willing to enter it only so far. What we must do is to get the other to talk— to communicate feelings—to get him to let us into his world as far as he is willing. As Buber says, "Entering into relation is an act of the whole being. It is the act by which we constitute ourselves as human."[6]

When I fail to listen actively—to "enter into relation" —I make your affective communication and your reality unavailable to me and to you as well. When I am unaware of your view of reality, I listen with about as much real understanding of you as I would have in listening to the language of a schizophrenic.

Another aspect of schizophrenic listening, then, is listening solely to the content of the speaker's message— his words—and ignoring his feelings, which contain his real or intended message. The roots of schizophrenic listening may, as we will see, be found as early as the neonatal period. But we can trace it at a later stage of development to the mistaken belief that there is an absolute reality; that only one way exists to "look at" a situation—one's own way.

Another explanation of schizophrenic listening concerns the difference between what family counselor Virginia Satir calls "connotative" and "denotative" messages.[7] The concept is similiar to that of Dr. Hayakawa. Connotative difficulties concern what words mean to different individuals. As an extreme example, among certain youth subcultures there was for awhile wide use of the word "bad" to characterize anything considered extremely good or desirable. I didn't know quite what to answer when, one day when I was wearing a new suit, a young man said, "That's a bad set of threads, man!"

Another and less extreme example is the word "manipulate." If I use that word in connection with a man's ability to do something, one person might understand me to mean that he has great dexterity; another might think I referred to his ability to use people to further his ends.

Denotative or content message difficulties have to do with differences in the meanings of words themselves. Those differences sometimes produce humorous results. A friend who is a writer sent me a copy of a magazine in which were published two of her works. Her note read, "I met the publisher of this magazine while on vacation. I told him about my poetry. He asked me to submit—so I did."

I sent a note by return mail to the effect that I had never thought her that sort of person, but that it was one way of getting into print which (so far as I knew, at least) was not open to me.

That story exemplifies another kind of complication: If my writer friend had been male, I would not have placed that particular denotation on the word "submit." Sex differences do add to the confusion.

In addition to the denotative level, there is also what psychologist and communication expert, Dr. Paul Watzlawick, has termed the "meta-level." A meta-communication or meta-message is a message about a message. You may have observed that most communication isn't communication at all. When people talk with each other, they generally talk about talking. Watzlawick points out the importance of the meta-message concept by stating that "Most, perhaps all, of the paradoxes encountered in mammalian communication are intimately linked to this level structure."[8]

The meta-message establishes the kind of relationship which exists between sender and receiver. Among wild animals, for example, the body language of the male establishes his role in the group. He may adopt a dominant or submissive stance, thus either reserving his right to lead the group and mate with the females or relinquishing those prerogatives to another male.

As another example, I customarily begin my first interview with a counselee by asking, "What is it that has brought you here?" The implication is that the client has some need or problem, and that I can somehow help this person meet the need or solve the problem. My words alone do not constitute the meta-message. My physical posture and attitude, the tone of voice with which I speak, and my facial expression—my nonverbal language—are also a part of it. I want the client to feel that I understand his desire for help, that I want to help, and that I can help. I also try to make it clear that I encourage him to share and that I am myself willing to share.

From that point I do my best to listen with the thought in mind that, as Watzlawick says, "message sent is not message received." In so doing I can use the relationship that my meta-message (and the client's) has established in order to listen in such a manner that he is willing to share his feelings. I can reduce the connotative and denotative differences between us. I can give feedback so that the client knows what message I have received and can correct me if I have not received the intended communication accurately. I can help him tap his view of reality in this way and lay it out for him to look at. I can help him sort out his alternatives so that he can choose from among them the one he feels will best meet his need. The important thing is that if my opening was successful, the client and I established a relationship in which there is understanding. Listening solidifies the relationship.

I mentioned earlier the importance of the content-feeling dichotomy, and we have seen an example of the way in which meta-messages establish relationships. Watzlawick makes a further refinement of message structure and defines a dichotomy which he calls "content-relationship."[9]

The relationships we establish can be of two types: symmetrical or complementary. In a symmetrical relationship each party considers himself equal to the other. In a complementary relationship one party will be in a one-up position and the other will be in a one-down position.

An example of a symmetrical relationship is seen in an adversary court proceeding where attorneys for the defense and prosecution try to outmaneuver one another and gain the one-up position. Junior executives competing for hegemony on the corporate ladder demonstrate another kind of symmetrical relationship.

Complementary relationships are quite common, exemplified by interactions between parent and young child, doctor and patient, and teacher and student. In each case it is the first member of the pair who is in the one-up position. The second member is quite willing to accept the one-down position.

Each of the two kinds of relationship has its advantages and problems. Symmetrical relationships can contain trust, sharing, and confidence. Although demanding equality of status, the parties to a symmetrical relationship have mutual respect for each other as individuals. But symmetry also breeds competitiveness; it implies that each party has rights, and it is the responsibility of each to see that the other gets his rights.

Complementary relationships have obvious advantages. A child's needs, for example, provide reason and purpose for the behavior of his parents. When the parties become locked into their respective roles as giver and receiver, however, the relationship can become frustratingly rigid.

What's needed is the ability to shift from one kind of relationship to the other in response to the feelings one senses. Parents, for instance, need to be sensitive to their child's growing desire to feel independent so that they know when to "let go." If they are schizophrenic listeners they won't have that sensitivity. They will fail to notice that their maturing offspring is no longer willing to play the one-down role on all occasions. The complementary-symmetrical conflict will reach an impasse. At that point communication will cease, and the all too familiar parent-teen brouhaha will result. The scene might be played something like this:

Mother has just informed her fifteen-year-old son that the family is going to grandmother's for the weekend.

"I'm not going," says Junior. "There's a big dance Saturday night, and I made plans to go."

"Well, you can forget about the dance. Your father and I decided you're going with us. We have no intention of leaving you home alone." (Mother is dealing solely with the content of her son's message.)

"Why don't you let *me* make a decision just once in my life! I'm not a baby, you know!" (The meta-message is that Junior wants a symmetrical relationship with his parents on this point. He's beginning to get a bit loud.)

"Don't raise your voice to me, young man!" (Mother is trying to maintain the one-up position.) "How can you talk to me that way after all I've done for you?" (Maybe guilt will do it.) Junior continues to push for symmetry.

"Look, Mom, I appreciate all the things you've done for me. I'd just like to do a few things for myself, like deciding about going to grandma's this weekend!"

And so it goes until (1) Mother wins, (2) Junior wins, or (3) the affair degenerates into a shouting match and everybody loses. All of this could have been avoided if Mom had really been listening and had heard her son's meta-message. Had she shifted the discussion to a symmetrical basis, things might have ended amicably. Junior might still have to go along to grandmother's—but when anger is eliminated from the exchange, there's a chance for them to negotiate a reasonable, no-lose settlement.

Complementary relationships provide room for give and take. It is only when father, mother, teacher, husband, son, child, student, or wife is willing to confirm the other's view of the relationship that it can continue to be a viable one. In order to be a father, for example, I need to get the kind of feedback from my son which indicates that he sees me as being a father. If he does not confirm me in that role, our father-son relationship does not exist.

The point is that any relationship between humans, whether symmetrical or complementary (and I'm not at all sure that these are the only choices), that involves speech also involves listening. Therefore, listening can have both a cause and an effect in determining whether a relationship develops, how it develops, and where it goes. If that father-son relationship flourishes, for instance, it's because real listening is taking place. It is safe to wager that if the relationship has broken down, somewhere along the way the father uttered words something like, "That boy refuses to listen to anything I tell him." The son has claimed, "I need somebody to talk to. My father won't listen to me." Each has been engaged in schizophrenic listening.

Now it probably isn't true that neither father nor son has ever listened to the other. What they mean is that the son has reached a point in his maturation where he's no longer willing to accept a position "inferior" to his father. The father, however, is unwilling to relinquish his role as giver. Each has lost his ability to view the relationship objectively. In fact the relationship itself is more important than their ability to communicate verbally, so they send destructive nonverbal messages. Similar examples can be drawn with other complementary pairs, and each could clearly show how preoccupation with relationship (or ignoring it) prevents listening.

Leonard and Natalie Zunin commented, "If every time

we met someone we gave him our full and complete attention for four minutes, come hell or high water, it could
change our lives."[10]

By "full and complete attention," Zunin and Zunin
mean a response which indicates to the other person that
we are really listening—not to what he is saying, but to
what makes him talk; and not from the standpoint of our
own reality so much as from his. To listen means to confirm the other's view of himself. To the degree we do that,
we can establish an enduring and satisfying relationship.
Alternative response styles will either deny the other's
existence or disconfirm his reality of himself. They are examples of schizophrenic listening.

Suppose, for example, that you are introduced to a
nuclear physicist. To you, that branch of science is fascinating. The conversation might go like this:

You: "Nuclear physics! My, you must find your work
very interesting and challenging." (That's a response based
on *your* view of reality.)

Physicist: "Not really. I used to enjoy research, but
now they've stuck me in the administrative end of it. I'm
just about ready to tell 'em to shove it!" (Your response
was obviously not consistent with his view of reality.)

But disconfirmation of another's reality is better than
an outright denial of his existence. Suppose that the conversation took this turn after your initial response:

Physicist: "Not really. I used to enjoy research, but
now they've stuck me in the administrative end of it. I'm
just about ready to tell 'em to shove it!"

You: "Say, isn't that Bob Smith over there?"

That kind of denial of another isn't calculated to win
you any friends. It's a good example of listening at its
worst: complete inattention.

Actually there's no way that you can avoid communicating. Even if you greeted the frustrated physicist's statement with complete silence, you would still be sending a
message. It wouldn't necessarily be the one you wanted to

send, though. Your silence may be construed as boredom, disinterest, sympathy, embarrassment, or irritation. The speaker may even think you're hard of hearing. Since you cannot *not communicate*, it's better to give a response you can control a bit better—a verbal one. But if it's not congruent, remember that the speaker may give more credence to your nonverbal response.

In any case your conversation with the physicist has opened with his response to your statement. The next move is up to you, and a lot depends on your next line. If you really listen and attend to what makes him talk, you'll be able to cultivate his friendship if that's what you wish. On the other hand, if you'd rather cut the relationship dead at this point, show him that you're a schizophrenic listener, that you're not really attending to the frustration that makes him talk. Show him that your mind is in flight from one associative thought of your own to another.

Not long ago I attended a lecture given by the noted marriage and family counselor, Dr. Howard Clinebell. He suddenly stopped in midsentence and asked, pointing to the microphone, "Is this thing turned on? Can you hear me?" When the audience nodded in the affirmative, Clinebell said, "O.K., good." Then as an afterthought he added, "Not that I'm suggesting that you *should* hear what I'm saying; I just wanted you to have the option."

I'm not suggesting that you should give everyone your complete attention or that you should befriend everyone to whom you're introduced. Perhaps schizophrenic listening is exactly what that crashing bore you met at the cocktail party deserves. But I want you to be aware that you have the option. The ability of really listening to others is an important skill. The exercise of economy in its use is an individual matter, one I will discuss in a later chapter.

To summarize thus far: we have seen that there are more good talkers than good listeners, and we have examined some poor listening styles. We have seen that there are times when one doesn't really want to be heard; times when one doesn't care whether one is heard or not; and times when one feels a desperate need to be heard. It's important to be able to distinguish among these different occasions within oneself—but it's even more important that one learn to recognize them within others.

I have discussed the three basic laws which govern communication: (1) one cannot *not communicate*, (2) the message sent by the speaker is not necessarily the message received by the listener, and (3) a communication consists of a message and a message about the message, or metamessage, which establishes the relationship between speaker and listener.

Schizophrenic listening directly results from the listener's failure to take into account the incongruity which may exist between the speaker's words and feeling, and between the speaker's and listener's views of reality. The situation is further complicated by the fact that the meanings of words used to convey the message are not in the words themselves—they are within the parties to the communication. This results in differences which have been termed connotative and denotative.

The schizophrenic listener attends solely to the speaker's words or message content. This has the effect of tending to make the speaker's reality unavailable not only to the listener but perhaps to the speaker as well. It also affects the direction of their relationship and can place a limit on its depth.

According to this theory, the style of the listener can create a symmetrical relationship in which each party views himself equal to the other, or a complementary one in which each party must confirm the other's view of his role. When a relationship becomes the overriding factor in communication, both parties lose their ability to look objectively at the communication and thus lose the ability to communicate. They begin to talk about talking. Thus we may now assume that we need to deal with two major facets of communication: content and feeling.

I conclude this chapter with one further example of the importance of listening. I recall attending a lecture presented by a prominent psychologist. His topic concerned communication within families, and he opened his talk with these words:

"I want to thank you for inviting me to address this distinguished gathering, and I am flattered that you feel I can add even a small bit to the considerable store of knowledge you represent. I am pleased to be able to make the attempt, but I cannot do it alone.

"Each of us has a job here this evening. Mine is to talk; yours is to listen. Here's what I'd like you to do. Should you get through with your job before I get through with mine, I would appreciate it if you would let me know."

2

The Language
of Schizophrenia

Chapter 1 dealt with the problem of schizophrenic listening, what it is, and why it interferes with communication. In this chapter we'll examine the model for schizophrenic listening, the language of the schizophrenic. Let's begin by reviewing two important factors in communication: feedback and conceptual sharing. Then we'll briefly explore some of the major linguistic theories and their application to normal and schizophrenic language.

Driving to my office a few mornings ago, I was listening to a San Francisco radio station. The news report had just concluded, and the engineer put a comedy album on the turntable. The premise of the particular excerpt being played was that someone had just telephoned the number listed for "Dial-a-Friend" and was not aware that the voice on the other end of the line was recorded. Implications of such a situation are obvious. The phone's receiver emits answers to questions which aren't asked and offers solutions to problems the caller doesn't have. The frustration of the caller can readily be imagined as his plea for help and understanding seems to fall on deaf ears.

But we can find the kinds of irritations presented in the "Dial-a-Friend" situation much closer to home. Have you ever encountered one of those fiendish electronic telephone-answering devices? I am always a bit disconcerted when one of those recorded voices replies. First, I feel odd conversing with a machine, and the result is an interruption in my train of thought. Then, while I'm trying to get the train back on the track, a "beep" in my ear informs me that the time allotted for recording my message has expired.

And have you ever attempted to explain to a police officer who just stopped you for running a stop sign that the traffic signal you failed to obey wasn't there yesterday? Or to the Internal Revenue Service auditor that the Hawaiian cruise you listed as a deductible expense was definitely taken for business reasons?

Each of these instances illustrates a situation in which one or both of the two important factors mentioned earlier —feedback and contextual sharing—are either lacking or inadequate. The phone-answering device provides an example of unilateral communication; a message was sent and perhaps received in full (if the caller was fast enough) —but *how* was it received? Because no provision exists for feedback, there's no way to verify the accuracy of the message reception.

In the case of the police officer and I.R.S. auditor, despite verbal feedback in response to your pleas, the outcome will probably be unpleasant to you. Why? Because that other important factor, contextual sharing, isn't there. Another reason is that the real feedback will come not in what these individuals say, but in what they do. Students of human communication generally agree that body language is a more reliable indicator of messages than is verbal language. Although reading body language takes study and practice, not much training is needed to understand the policeman's intent when he hands you a citation, or the auditor's when he gives you a paper indicating underpayment of your tax.

Of course there are times when verbal feedback is not only unnecessary but really not wanted at all. Take that fellow on the subway this morning. As he held onto the overhead strap to keep from being hurled to the floor, he looked up from his newspaper just in time to catch that attractive young lady across the aisle watching him. He smiled; she smiled back as their eyes met; then both quickly looked away. As the train continued its lurching journey, they both cast a few more surreptitious glances. Three stops further the interlude ended as the cars slammed to a halt and disgorged them along with a score of other commuters. The young lady and gentlemen had both enjoyed the fantasy of a moment of nonverbal interchange—much more, perhaps, than they would have enjoyed the reality of verbal feedback.

The point is that, even at the very lowest levels of communication, a response to a message is necessary, whether the message is expressed verbally or nonverbally. The response or feedback may also be verbal or nonverbal, and it must be a response in which sender and receiver share the same contextual referent. For reasons we have seen in chapter 1, it is impossible for both to have precisely the same view of the context in which their communications occur. But even with differing views of it, they must recognize that the context is actually the same. For example, let's look again at the foregoing illustrations.

In the "Dial-a-Friend" comedy bit, obviously there was no meeting of minds about context, since one voice was recorded. The same is true of the telephone-answering device, although contextual sharing in that case is somewhat closer. Unless the caller dialed a wrong number, some common ground must exist between him and the owner of the electronic gadget. The police officer certainly shares the same context as the hapless motorist about to receive a citation. What the two don't share is a common view of the situation. That eagle-eyed income tax man and the harried taxpayer likewise see themselves as being in the same context, but they disagree strongly with regard to the realities of the context. And what about the gentleman and his paramour-in-fantasy on the subway? The fact that neither can know the other's view of the context at the moment makes the fantasy possible. It's the bliss of ignorance— something like the feeling of proud parents who assume that their offspring has just bestowed upon them his first smile. They'd just as soon not know that it was actually a grimace of pain due to colic.

In some respects each foregoing example illustrates a similarity to attempting conversation with a schizophrenic. Certainly the net result of each is comparable. In the speech of the schizophrenic the factors of comprehensible feedback and contextual sharing are either missing or unavailable to the listener. Without them the schizophrenic's messages—or the normal individual's, for that matter—become incomprehensible. It isn't clear whether the schizophrenic makes an honest attempt to share his context and provide comprehensible feedback. Possibly, consciously or unconsciously, his messages are designed to be unclear. Whether or not conscious or unconscious motivational influence exists, however, the effect is the same.

But suppose the parties to a communication—or at least to an intended one—honestly attempt to provide comprehensible feedback and to share their contextual views, and fail? What if the views of the communicators are so far removed from each other that meaningful feedback becomes impossible?

A new field of study called "psycholinguistics" has begun to shed light on such complexities. Psycholinguistics is an approach to the study of language which blends theories about language with the empirical tools of psychology. The major purpose of psycholinguistics is to study the psychological processes involved in acquiring and using language. With the advent of this new approach some well-established notions about language are being observed in a new light. For example, one such long-held idea is the already mentioned question of unconscious motivational factors. In the psychoanalytic view unconscious motivation does influence the comprehensibility of language. But psycholinguists are no longer altogether convinced that this is true.

Of greater interest today are psycholinguistic factors which seem to contribute to normal comprehensible language. One finding of particular concern to us here is that some of the psycholinguistic skills or abilities which normal individuals generally possess to an adequate degree appear to be absent or at least deficient among schizophrenics. Specifically, the schizophrenic shows deficits in short-term memory, attention span, and ability to process information. As applied to our goal of improving listening skills, that's a very important finding indeed. Why? Well, before you begin to feel superior you should know that not only the schizophrenic has these deficiencies. Although schizophrenics manifest them to a pathological degree, we who are otherwise normal exhibit those same deficits to a lesser degree. It's not that we don't have the skills; we just don't use them. We'll take a closer look at those findings a bit later, with special attention as to how they affect communication. But bear in mind that what follows applies, to a degree, not only to schizophrenics but to you and me as well.

Let's look now at some of the major psychological and linguistic theories so that we'll have a firm base for what's to come. Before we can become really skilled listeners, we'll need to know more about our own psycholinguistic workings. Especially important is how and why they may compare with those of the schizophrenic. For example, what's the connection, if any, between what we think and what we say? Have you ever had the experience of asking yourself, immediately after putting your verbal foot in your mouth, "Now why did I say that?"

When man began to consider what a wondrous creature he was, one of his first philosophical interests quite fittingly was his language. For centuries he thought that only he of all creatures on earth had the ability to communicate intelligently. But researchers are beginning to prove the shortsightedness of that opinion. For example, psychologists Allen and Beatrice Gardner of the University of Nevada have taught a chimpanzee named "Washoe" to communicate in American Sign Language.[1]

Among the questions philosophers pondered with regard to man's means of communication was whether or not a connection existed between thought and speech. Were they one and the same? Or were speech and thought separate from each other? During the many centuries since those early wonderings, convincing arguments have been generated on both sides of the issue. But there is still no definitive answer. Positions range along a continuum from an unqualified *yes, they are one and the same* to an unqualified *no, they are not.*

One of those who saw no connection between the two was John Broadus Watson, father of American behavioristic psychology. Watson proposed an explanation which quite predictably accorded with the stimulus-response theory of behavior. He stated that thought processes are actually learned behaviors centered in the musculature of the larynx. Speech, Watson insisted, was nothing more than audible thought, and thought was nothing more than covert speech.[2]

I remember a sign on the wall of a colleague's office that read, "Please do not start mouth until brain is engaged." Whoever wrote that was not a Watsonian behaviorist. Another familiar line is the one about some unknown individual who "started his mouth and then walked off and left it going." That sounds more like applied American behaviorism. I wager that each of us has encountered individuals who rattle on in mechanical fashion without any discernible thought behind their words.

Not all behaviorists completely agreed with Watson, however. One who disagreed was a Russian named Ivan M. Sechenov. A physiologist, Sechenov was Pavlov's teacher.

He argued that while it was true that speech and thought are closely linked in childhood, they lose that close link as the human develops. According to Sechenov's theory, man as adult is able to think without connection to speech—overt or covert.[3]

In Geneva, Jean Piaget, the noted Swiss developmental psychologist, advanced another theory in complete disagreement with the behaviorist view. Piaget's position is that cognitive development follows its own laws during childhood. Generally, he says, language develops consequent to the development of thought processes. According to Piaget, while speech may serve to amplify and extend intellectual processes, it doesn't significantly contribute to the formation of intellectual processes.[4]

Whether thought and speech are unrelated or partially related, or whether speech depends upon thought or vice versa, remains to be decided. For practical purposes, what matters is that man is normally capable of transmitting messages which are comprehensible because they seem to reflect his thoughts.

Another concern germane to us is the interest of increasing numbers of researchers in the degree of language comprehensibility. Normal speech contains redundancies. That is to say, it's possible to delete parts of utterances without adverse effect on the listener's ability to comprehend the speaker's message—or at least the content thereof. An exaggerated example is the story about the fish peddler who wanted to make a sign for his stand. His initial effort resulted in a sign which read, "Fresh fish for sale today." His helpful friend observed that the sign contained unnecessary words. The word "today" certainly wasn't necessary, since that would be obvious to potential customers. And why "for sale"? Why else would the peddler set up a stand in the marketplace? Whether the fish were fresh, the friend insisted, was more a matter for nose than eyes. For that matter, any interested customer could see for himself that the commodity offered was fish without benefit of a sign to that effect.

As already admitted, that bit of nonsense is an exaggeration of the redundance principle; moreover, it's quite remote from its research counterpart. But it does illustrate the idea that a word's degree of redundancy in a message may be measured by its probability of occurrence. Only a head count of customers would determine whether the fish peddler would have been more successful with his original sign than with no sign. Notwithstanding that conjecture, however, redundancy is an important means of increasing comprehensibility because it serves as a repetition of the message. The more repetitive the message, the greater its comprehensibility.

The connection between redundancy and comprehensibility is the basis for a device known as the "Cloze procedure," which is used for estimating the redundancy of language. It involves the elimination of words from written material at intervals. Every fifth word, for instance, may be left out. A group of readers given copies of the altered text is asked to guess the missing words. The more words the group can guess correctly, the more redundant and hence the more comprehensible the text.

Investigators using the Cloze procedure have found that the language of schizophrenics has a low degree of redundancy. Several theories also applicable to normal individuals have been advanced to explain this phenomenon. One of them sees the schizophrenic as a person who, in effect, doesn't know what's coming next in his speech because he literally pays no attention to what he has just said. Could that explain the "Now why did I say that?" experience?

Psychologist Paul Watzlawick has another theory. He suggests that the schizophrenic has not resigned himself to the undeniable fact that one cannot *not communicate*. He must therefore deny that he is communicating. But his denial is itself a communication, and it too must be denied. The schizophrenic, as Watzlawick sees him, fears two things about communication. First, he's afraid to let the listener know what his message is about; and second, he's afraid to let the listener know how he sees the relationship between himself and the listener. His fear is based on his past experiences in which either disclosure resulted in his being made to feel he had done something reprehensible.

As an example, Watzlawick presents a situation in which an alcoholic father demands that his children see him as a loving, respectable parent. The father knows that he's actually a violent drunkard. He threatens to punish his children if they show fear when he comes home drunk. The children are thus forced to deny their fear and their own perceptions of their relationship with him.[5] The father is successful at forcing this denial on his children. Then he suddenly reverses his position and accuses them of lying to him about their fear. They are now in what researcher Gregory Bateson has termed a "double-bind."[6] If they show that they fear him, he will punish them for implying he's a violent drunkard. If they hide their fear, he'll punish them for being liars. Thus to communicate is to be punished, and not to communicate is impossible. The result is schizophrenic language.

Another possible mechanism which may account for the incomprehensible speech of the schizophrenic is association. Brendan Maher holds that the key to schizophrenic language is associative chaining. We noted that the schizophrenic manifests a deficit in attention span. Maher says that because of the schizophrenic's difficulty in maintaining attention, associations intrude themselves in his speech when his attention lapses. Here's how Maher illustrates the situation.

First, here is the schizophrenic's sentence as it was intended to be: "I have pains in my chest and wonder if there is something wrong with my heart." Now let's look at the same sentence with the associative intrusions: "I have pains (aches; doctor) in my chest (box; trunk) and wonder (hope) if there is something wrong (right; bad; failure) with my heart (beat; soul; save; heaven; broken)."

Now, here's the sentence as it was actually uttered: "Doctor, I have pains in my chest and hope and wonder if my box is broken and heart is beaten for my soul and salvation and heaven, Amen."[7]

Maher has also found that schizophrenic patients are deficient in the ability to use context cues to determine meanings of ambiguous words. For example, where the normal individual would be able to tell which meaning of the word "bar" applies in the sentence "Jones passed the bar examination last week," the schizophrenic would not. Similarly, from a group of words such as "alcohol, glass, bar," the normal person would probably be able to define "bar" as a place to get a drink.

Aside from poor attention and the associative chaining which, Maher theorizes, pair together to cause the characteristically incomprehensible speech of the schizophrenic, Yates hypothesizes another kind of pathology, to which Maher refers. According to Australian psychologist Yates, schizophrenics have a deficiency in short-term storage processes and recall. Yates regards this deficiency as a slowing of the rate at which incoming messages are processed. The short-term memory system is, in effect, overloaded to such an extent that information is lost and never committed to long-term memory. Yates' hypothesis is not yet adequately supported by experimental data. It is, however, consistent with descriptions given of their difficulties by schizophrenic patients. There is also statistically significant evidence that such patients perform better on tasks that involve information processing if the information is presented at a slow rate.[8]

The idea that the language of the schizophrenic may be understood by analysis of his associations has also been suggested by Julius Laffal. Like Maher, Laffal assumes that the language of schizophrenics contains words that enter into utterance because of their association with other words in the utterance. But Laffal believes this true for the normal speaker as well. The concept is reminiscent of Freudian association. By listing a particular word, then listing other words that tend to appear whenever that word is used by the speaker, some idea of the psychological significance of the word may be obtained.

Despite the absence of any clear connection between a given word and the words that appear with it, Laffal thinks that an important association exists even though that association may not be recognized by the speaker. In schizophrenics the intrusive associations become more evident and render the speaker's message incoherent.[9]

Thus far we have considered the language of the schizophrenic as abnormal. That's the orthodox view: schizophrenic language is an absurd response to a normal situation. But perhaps the real situation is just the reverse. Perhaps schizophrenic language is a completely appropriate response to an absurd situation. Let's go back for a moment to Watzlawick's double-bind example of the alcoholic father. Watzlawick suggests that the situation might be seen as resulting from the following:

1. Satisfactory relationships can only exist where communication is clear. One must be able to say what he means and to understand what others mean when they relate to him. In the absence of this, he is not only unable to understand another; he is also unable to understand himself.
2. One cannot act on his understanding of a communication when any indication that his understanding is correct brings the threat of punishment.
3. The threat of punishment will be conveyed by the speaker if he himself is unable to accept the actual meaning of his message. He

may convey the threat verbally or non-verbally.[10]

To review, the language of the schizophrenic appears to make sense to him. It seems to be based on his own view of reality, and intrusive associations or disruptions only serve to make his message unclear to the listener. Only one who has studied such language is able to decipher its meaning because the processes by which normal individuals clarify their own and others' messages are absent or deficient in schizophrenics. On the other hand the schizophrenic has difficulty comprehending the messages of others because his processing of incoming language is deficient. Because his short-term memory is inadequate, he's unable to receive language at a normal rate. As a result he loses much information because it never gets into his long-term storage/retrieval system. The problem is much like trying to force a liquid to run through a funnel at a faster rate than the diameter of the funnel's throat will permit.

Other factors in blocking comprehensible communication include those of missing or inadequate feedback and the impossibility of sharing identical views of the context of communication.

Up to this point I've discussed the problem of schizophrenic language from the standpoint of the speaker's inability to supply comprehensible messages. But the problem of schizophrenic language is not so much the speaker's as the listener's. If we may assume that the schizophrenic's speech makes sense to himself and taps his own reality, then the difficulty of communication lies in the inability of the listener to "get inside" the schizophrenic's reality. For all practical purposes we might say that it isn't schizophrenic speech which is blocking comprehension, but schizophrenic listening; and we should look in that direction.

There are other reasons for turning our attention to the listener rather than the speaker. First, it's the listening process and aberrations thereof which form the major focus of our interest in this book. Listening, after all, is under our control as listeners, at least to the degree that we are normal. The performance of the speaker is beyond our control, and we can know very little about his internal processes. His utterances are cognitively determined by what he wants the listener to know, not by what the listener expects he will say. Not all psycholinguists would agree with that latter statement, but we will assume that it is so.

As we proceed to chapter 3, remember that everything said thus far in regard to schizophrenic communication applies in lesser degree to normal communication.

*Usually, a person relates to another under
the tacit assumption that the other shares
his view of reality, that, indeed, there
is only one reality. . . .*   Paul Watzlawick

3

Exploring Some Dynamics of Schizophrenic Listening

Simply because a person thinks he knows himself, he frequently assumes that he knows others. We sometimes use the expression "To know what I mean you've got to know where I'm coming from." To illustrate that point the following short story, which I shall title "Analog," is presented. Your task is to determine what it means.

Once upon a time there was a village of Wise Men. The village was named Knowledge, for that was the name given by the Elders of the village, and it was located far upstream on the bank of the great river known as the River of Truth.

The Wise Men were held in great respect by all the inhabitants of the many villages which lined the banks of the River of Truth downstream from the Village of Knowledge, for the Wise Men had a very special gift.

In the crystal waters of the peaceful river lived a particular fish on which all the villagers depended. The properties of the fish were truly marvelous, as it provided sustenance and the means of procreating the race of villagers.

35

But the fish were useful for neither purpose in their natural state. And the Wise Men of the Village of Knowledge had gained adulation and livelihood from the fact that only they among all men had been chosen to render the fish useful. Only they had been given the ability to train the fish. From a point of beginning long since forgotten it had always been so—the Wise Men performing their wonders on the fish and the other villagers reaping the benefits—and, in exchange, showering the Wise Men with admiration and material gifts.

Then, so gradually that it went undiscovered for a long time, the pleasant balance between the Village of Knowledge and the other villages along the River of Truth began to change.

The first evidence was manifest, had not complacency fogged the vision of the Wise Men, in the almost imperceptible clouding of the river's crystal waters. This the Elders and Councils of Wise Men reconstructed as they sat about their fires on the long nights following the increasingly difficult days of labor along the riverbank; and they also became aware, little by little, of other strange happenings.

As the river grew more and more murky, it seemed that the numbers of fish were decreasing too, and what fish remained now began behaving in strange, unaccustomed ways. For example, the fish did not, as in ages past, swim straight for the waiting nets on the banks of the Village of Knowledge. Instead they gathered in separate groups, each group characterized by a slightly different manner of moving through the water. This the Wise Men could not explain nor had they ever seen such differences.

Moreover, the groups of fish were openly hostile toward one another and appeared to be avoiding the Wise Men. Many of the fish did not even remain long enough to be fully trained in the waters near the Village of Knowledge, but instead swam downstream toward the other villages—where, useless to the villagers, they swam about near the shores of the River of Truth just outside the strong current of the Mainstream.

"This is incredible!" muttered the Elders and the Wise Men at their fireside councils. "What can the fish be thinking of?" Thus they pondered angrily, forgetting a fact learned from their forebears. The fish which traveled down the River of Truth had no power of thought; only the Wise Men among all the creatures of Earth had that.

The troubles of the Wise Men of Knowledge continued to worsen slowly but inexorably. The villagers downstream who depended on the Wise Men began to grumble as they felt the results of the shortage of fish, and they no longer held the Wise Men in such high esteem. They sent delegations, an unheard-of action, to visit Knowledge and investigate the situation. The delegations took the Elders and Wise Men to task and demanded immediate action, then left in frustration; for neither the Elders nor the Wise Men could explain the change of affairs.

"You must do as we," the people of Knowledge told the other villagers, "wait and hope. Surely the nadir has been reached." But next morning they were to learn that they were mistaken.

Soon after most of the Wise Men had gone to the river for their daily labor, one of their number came racing through the village screaming unintelligibly, in obvious fright. He beckoned the rest of the Wise Men and Elders to follow him, which they did.

What they beheld upon arriving at the river struck fear in the hearts of all. There, just to one side of the Mainstream of the River of Truth, stood a cluster of their fellows huddled in terror. All about them were gathered groups of fish, hardly distinguishable in the now almost opaque water. The fish had thus far made no move, but their intent as they slowly circled was clear. The formerly separate and mutually antagonistic group of fish had now united in their hostility toward their erstwhile trainers.

Finding themselves in such bewildering and horrifying

straits, all the Wise Men stood frozen for a moment. Then, with the Elders remaining behind to shout support, those on the shore waded almost as one into the river in a show of force. Not one of them knew or had even guessed what damage the fish might inflict; and they watched with great relief as the groups of fish dispersed and swam off.

That night the fires burned long. The threatened attack, said a scattering of Wise Men, required some kind of definitive action. Perhaps if they tried to work cooperatively with the fish . . . but they were voted down by the Elders, who maintained unyieldingly that the best thing to do was wait.

"We must try to find out why the behavior of the fish has changed," said another few. "Perhaps different ways of training are required for these new fish."

"Nonsense," insisted the Elders, "this will pass if we are patient. We will continue to train them as did our fathers and their fathers before them. It is the only way."

Another minority suggested, "Perhaps we should seek out the reason for the murkiness of the river. Perhaps the reason for that and the mysterious change in the behavior of the fish have a connection."

All except the Elders greeted this recommendation with murmurs of approval and sage nodding of heads; for it was then that the Wise Men realized they had never visited the source of the River of Truth. For the first time in the known history of the village called Knowledge, a majority of Wise Men voted to disregard the advice of the Elders and commended those who had made the suggestion.

"We will find out where the River of Truth begins its journey, and we will learn through what diverse regions the fish must pass before they reach our village."

So saying and satisfied with their intentions, they slept.

But they were too late. In the cold predawn light of the following morning, as the Village of Knowledge lay locked in the last moments of deep slumber, the fish emerged from the River of Truth and slew all of the Wise Men.

When the Elders awoke and witnessed the carnage, they admonished the lifeless bodies: "If only you had listened to us and simply waited!"

The next morning the fish returned and slew the Elders.

Were you able to figure out what I meant (where I was coming from) when I wrote that story? Except by wildest chance, that would be impossible for you to do. It would be equally impossible for me to determine what meaning the story holds for you because I have no way of knowing where you were coming from when you read it. We would first have to sit down together and establish a frame of reference—in other words, communicate. Only then could you possibly understand my meaning and I yours.

Unfortunately, although that same principle applies to our daily conversations with others, it is frequently— perhaps usually—ignored. When we are told something, we assume that the meaning of the words—the message—is clear, and we presuppose a mutual frame of reference. That point was made in the previous chapters. But there's another point here, as well.

When we hear or think we hear what others tell us, we often interpret what we think they have said with the assumption that we not only understand others, but that we understand ourselves too. In other words we assume that we understand others because we assume that we understand ourselves. But few of us truly have self-understanding; and even if we do, understanding one's self does not necessarily lead to effective listening or to clear communication because it is not only self-understanding which we must concern ourselves with as listeners and communicators, but our relationship with the speaker also.

Thomas Hora put it this way: "To understand himself

man needs to be understood by another. To be understood by another he needs to understand the other."[1]

Understanding, then, presupposes that communication has taken place between speaker and listener. For example, one often doesn't really understand the meaning of his own messages until they are fed back to him by another. But that other cannot know whether his feedback is accurately reflecting the speaker's intent unless the speaker, in turn, gives him feedback. Continual give-and-take testing of one's understanding of what he has heard and the accuracy of his interpretation is necessary for effective communication. In my experience that kind of testing seldom occurs, and rarely are the results as clearly evident as within family units. Since such testing is an important factor in correcting schizophrenic listening, let's take a closer look at what can happen to family relationships when feedback is absent.

The more I work with families, the more I find that problems frequently center around one of two difficulties: (1) the family members think they *are* communicating when they're not, or (2) the family members think they are *not* communicating when they are.

The first difficulty is a quite common one. It occurs when one member of the family says something which doesn't accurately convey to the other(s) his feelings at that moment. The response he gets as a result may reflect the content of his statement, but the feelings and emotions behind the content remain bottled up. They will surface then or later, probably in a way which will cause disharmony in the family.

Consider as an example the following vignette:

Dad comes home from work half an hour later than usual. He walks in the door and announces, "I'm fed up with that kid, Mary. I left explicit orders that the front lawn was to be mowed this afternoon when he got home from school!"

What is really on his mind is something like this: "I'm

mad as hell at my boss. At the last minute he came in and gave me work that he should have done. Then he went home and I had to work overtime. I feel like telling him off!"

But Mom is angry too. Her painstakingly prepared dinner is cold, so she doesn't hear Dad's true feelings being expressed. She replies, "At least you could say hello when you come in the door instead of jumping all over me about the lawn. I wasn't supposed to mow it, so don't take it out on me. Talk to Junior. He was the one you told to do it!"

What is really on *her* mind is this: "I'm really upset. Doctor Smith told me this afternoon that he found a suspicious spot on my x-rays, and I have to go into the hospital next week for tests."

Because of his anger at his boss, Dad didn't get the feeling behind Mom's words. He turns on his heel and heads upstairs toward his son's room, shouting at the top of his voice, "Junior! I want to talk to you! Come down here! And turn off that damned music! I don't know how you can listen to that noise!"

Instead of Junior, Sis comes to the head of the stairs.

"Junior isn't home yet, Daddy. He had to stay at school this afternoon. The coach called a special practice session."

Father doesn't know quite what to say at this point, but his anger is still pent up so he can't see his way clear to apologize. Instead he storms out of the house, leaving behind a hurt and bewildered Sis and a distraught, crying wife. He gets into the car and aims it toward the nearest bar.

That scene is an example of the first communication difficulty. Both parents thought they were communicating, and neither was. But that difficulty can be avoided. Let's play the same scene again; but this time the parents will really communicate.

Father comes in the door, kisses his wife and says, "Sorry I'm late again, Mary. It was my boss. I'm really angry with him. At the last minute he shoved one of his assignments off onto me and he went home. It wouldn't be so bad if I was getting extra pay, but I'm not."

Mother answers, "It sounds as though you're fed up and feel you're being taken unfair advantage of."

"Yeah, that's exactly it, Mary."

"I'll bet you'd like a chance just to relax a bit before dinner. Sis has already eaten, so I'll put our dinner in the oven. If you'd like to fix a drink, I'll join you."

As Father heads for the kitchen, Mom calls upstairs.

"Sis, your Father's home. And would you please turn down your radio."

"Sure, Mom!" Sis comes bouncing down the stairs to greet her father and gives him a peck on the cheek. "Hi, Dad. See you later. I'm going over to Joan's to study."

As Mom joins Dad in the kitchen, she says, 'Oh, I nearly forgot. Junior had football practice, so he couldn't cut the lawn this afternoon. He promised he'd cut it tomorrow."

"Oh," Dad replies. "I wondered about that. O.K., it'll keep 'til tomorrow. How was your day, Mary? Everything go all right at the doctor's?"

"Not really. He found something on my x-rays. He said it's probably nothing, but just to be on the safe side he wants to run some tests."

"Sounds like you're optimistic about the tests."

"Well, yes, but I'm still a bit apprehensive."

I'm sure you see the difference. Communication is a three-step process. When you're really communicating, you make your message concrete enough so that it's clear and accurately describes your feelings at the moment.

That's your step-1 obligation as a communicator. The key is your use of the personal pronoun "I". *I* feel upset, *I'm* angry, *I'm* worried, etc; and a statement that tells as much as possible about who, what, where, when, why and how. You'd soon become frustrated with someone who failed to communicate specifics—if he reported, for example, that "Somebody told me that somewhere in one of the southern states a bunch of people did something today."

The listener also has an obligation to be a communicator. He must provide feedback, a response that lets the speaker know how his message has been heard. That's step 2.

In step 3 the speaker affirms the accuracy of the listener's feedback or corrects any errors by restating the message for the listener. This three-phase process continues until the speaker is satisfied that the message received by the listener was the message he sent. We'll return to this process later.

Now let's get back to the second difficulty, the one which results from members communicating when they think they are not. Here's an example of what I mean:

Father has called home to tell Mother he will be a half-hour late. He can tell by her tone of voice that she's unhappy. What he doesn't know is that she has spent hours preparing his favorite meal which must be served when it's ready. When he called, it was ready. Even though Mother didn't mean to communicate her unhappiness, she did. But Father misinterpreted her tone of voice as irritation. As he hangs up the phone he thinks "I don't know what *she's* mad about. I'm the one who has to work late. She must think I enjoy being taken advantage of by my boss. At least I called to let her know."

As he returns to his work his feeling of being unfairly treated by his wife grows into minor anger, and by the time he arrives home his anger is full-blown. He walks into the house and makes straight for the liquor cabinet as Mom comes out of the kitchen.

"Hello, dear," she offers.

"Humph," he grunts, not even looking at her.

"Are you angry about something?"

"No," he lies. "Where's the paper?"

Now Mom is beginning to feel angry. Without communicating it in words Dad has told her that he's angry with her. She thinks to herself "I don't know what right *he* has to be angry with me. I'm the one who prepared the dinner that's now a disaster because he was late!"

She retreats to the kitchen while he seeks refuge behind the evening paper. Dinner is served in silence and eaten under a cloud of hostility which neither has described. This too could have been avoided. For instance, when he called Mother, Dad might have said, "You sound as though you're angry." Mother could have replied, "No, I'm not angry. I'm just a little disappointed that your favorite dinner won't be the way I want it to be."

The point is that unspoken messages are just as communicative as spoken ones, and they too need the three-step communication process. In either case the speaker wants to convey a feeling, and the listener must help him do it accurately and clearly. But what happens if the speaker deliberately tries to hide his true feelings—avoids letting the listener know just who he is and where he's coming from? This happens more often than not in interactions.

As a child you probably played a game called "hide-and-seek." In that game most of the children would hide, and the one designated as being "it" would then try to find them. As "it" endeavored to locate the places of concealment he would call out, "Come out, come out, wherever you are!" The first person found then became "it," and the game proceeded as the new "it" covered his eyes while new hiding places were chosen.

As adults we play a similar game in which "it" calls "Come out, come out, *whoever* you are!" The rules of the game are quite unlike the childhood model. They vary from individual to individual, each of us making up his own on the basis of a variety of criteria which I will discuss. Nevertheless, the idea is the same, and like "hide-and-seek," this adult game is quite well rooted in history.

In the ancient Greek theater the players wore painted masks to portray the emotions of the characters they

This receipt is your official notice of the due dates of the items you have checked out. Any email or phone reminders are for convenience only. All items not returned or renewed by the specified dates will be subject to fines.

DATE DUE RECEIPT

User name: **NEAL-VINCENT, JANICE**
Title: How to listen, how to be heard
Author: Banville, Thomas G.
Item ID: 31776000501302
Date due: 1/28/2015,23:59

played. Since there were more parts than actors, each new character only required a change of masks. The personality of the actor was not permitted to intrude into the play. This concept has continued to be the norm. The mask, in a sense, is still used. In fact the word "personality" derives from the Latin *per sonare*, meaning "to speak through," referring to the mask behind which the actor spoke. With the evolution of modern theater, the actor quite literally became the character he played. Signs, for instance, advertised that "Paul Newman *is* Hud."

The difference between the actor as actor and the actor as person is often startling, however. Late-night talk shows provide insights into these differences. Just the other evening I witnessed one of our finest character actors, who is extremely articulate and apparently completely at ease on the screen, dissolve into an inarticulate, mumbling blob obviously wishing himself anywhere but there at that moment.

Although some actors no doubt practiced the principles of Method acting long before, not until that school made its formal debut did the actor's feelings not only become congruent with those of the character being played, but even dominated them. Since the Method apparently requires an empathic relationship between the actor and the character he portrays, feelings are shared. But although the face and feelings of the actor are no longer concealed behind a mask, his character often is. Like the ancient Greek, even the Method actor often hides behind the character he portrays.

Writer David Fowler asks, "How many yous are there? Fifteen? Ten? Three? Maybe there's the deep you or the humorous you, or the blue you, the perceptive you, or maybe you've found a you that even you don't really know."[2]

You and I, the Greek and the Method actor all operate inside that closed system mentioned earlier. The real person hides behind a mask or a character. His own feelings are not allowed to surface. The role is the dominant factor.

For most of us interpersonal relationships involve role playing. We behave in accordance with how we would like to be seen or how we think we should be seen rather than how we actually are. For each different other person and in each different situation we select the mask—the "you" —which our self-concept and experience dictate as appropriate. The role is played against a backdrop of values, morals, conscience, "tapes," "role constructs," or "scripts." Sometimes there are so many roles to play, so many "you's" that selecting the "right" one from the repertoire becomes difficult. It's this search for the "you" to present in any given situation that prevents one from understanding the other person and thus from understanding himself.

Frederick Perls described the phenomenon in these words: "The crazy person says, 'I am Abraham Lincoln,' and the neurotic says, 'I wish I were Abraham Lincoln,' and the healthy person says, 'I am I and you are you.' "[3] The submergence of self to which Perls alludes may be seen rather clearly in marriages that begin to falter. In effect the partners say, "I am I because you are you, and you are you because I am I." When the partners become nothing more than reflections of each other, the marriage dies. A divorced person whose identity has been thus submerged will probably rush out and marry someone exactly like the spouse that was just shed, and the process begins all over again.

Psychologist Carl Whitaker suggests that loss of self begins during the courting period and is manifested in such statements as "I can't live without you." Whitaker says that divorce should be followed by a period of what he terms "decourting." During the decourting period the former spouse works at becoming a person in his or her own right and tries to regain a sense of self-identity.[4] The question is, what self—what "you"—will one identify with? In order to answer that, one must know who and what one is; and, more to the present point, how one got that way. That requires openness, a willingness to share and disclose one's self. And that openness and sharing is something each of us needs in order to become a more effective listener and a better communicator.

In this chapter we saw the impossibility of understanding the meaning of another person's message without having available his frame of reference. We have also examined the assumption that one can understand oneself without understanding another and the mistaken notion that self-understanding is synonymous with effective listening and clear communication. We have looked rather closely at two kinds of communication failure and how they can affect interactions among family members. Illustrations were presented of how those communication failures might be corrected.

Finally there was a brief discussion of the tendency to hide one's self and one's true feelings, which will serve to introduce chapter 4—where we will treat in depth the sharing of feelings and why that sharing is necessary to effective communication and listening.

We begin now to enter the part of this book in which you'll begin to work on changing your own listening style. So that you'll be able to look back later and see your progress, let's pause here for a sample of your present styles of listening and response.

I will present several communications that you might hear expressed in certain situations. Read each of them carefully but only once. Then write the reply you would normally give if someone uttered them to you. Place the paper with you responses in the pages of this book so that you can locate it later when I ask you to do so.

1. "I can't figure out what's wrong, but lately I've had a tough time getting up during the week. On Saturday and Sunday when I *could* sleep later, I'm up at the crack of dawn!"
2. "I just finished reading that new best seller

you recommended. Frankly I thought it was very amateurish. The characters were poorly drawn, and the plot was only so-so. Did you really like it?"

3. "You know, of all the people I've ever met, Joe is the nicest. I don't recall that he has ever said an unkind word about anyone. On the other hand, his wife is a real bitch. I don't know what in the world he ever saw in her."

4. "Remember that opening I said was coming up in my company's home office? Well, what do you think—they asked me if I wanted it. It's a great chance to move up the ladder, but ... I don't know, we have so many ties here; our new home, and the kids love the school ... I'm not sure how Bill would take it."

4

To Be That Self
Which One Truly Is

To be able to be what we inly are and to be free to show it is most certainly something to mark with light in one's memory. As adults few of us are permitted that freedom by others, few permit it of themselves, and few permit it of others. More than a century ago Kierkegaard, the Danish philosopher, wrote that the deepest form of despair is to choose to be someone other than one's self; but the opposite of despair is to will to be that self which one truly is.

Of all stages in human development only the socially uninitiated infant discloses himself to the world as he really is. At that point of his life man is as close to being a pure product of his genetic inheritance as he will ever be, since he is virtually untouched by environmental influences. The further removed he is from infancy, the less he tends toward self-disclosure.

A friend who is a music specialist for a school system once remarked that something seemed to happen to children when they reached the fourth grade. In the first three grades, she observed that during vocal music lessons the youngsters joined with gusto, singing at the top of their voices. But by the time they entered fourth grade at nine years of age, their spontaneity was gone. Inhibition had appeared—not in all the children, certainly, but in many of them. They became unable or unwilling to share with others this particular part of themselves.

In later chapters we will examine the processes by which inhibitions develop and what can be done to reduce their effects. Right now we'll concern ourselves with the role that restriction or nonsharing of feelings plays in schizophrenic listening.

Failure in human interrelationships can often be traced to our desire to be understood on our own terms. We tend to present to others only that information about ourselves which we care—or dare—to let them know. For most of us the information is restricted to those things which present us in what we presume to be the best light, and which are consistent with our idea of what we *should* be like. For the same reasons we inhibit behaviors which would reveal our true feelings. In Thomas Hora's terms, this means that since we never allow ourselves to be truly understood by another, we never come to understand ourselves.[1] Thus, even more crucial to our interpersonal relationships, we never become able to understand others.

Psychiatrists have described the difference between insanity and sanity as the difference between constantly pleading, "Somebody please love me" and constantly searching for someone to whom one can give love. The insane group consists of those who seek to be understood and loved. These are the schizophrenic listeners of the world. In relationships, they are unable to accept (and thus never deal with) others' self-revelations, and they are unable to reveal themselves.

Love requires an open relationship between the lovers —one in which there is freedom to express feelings. In such a relationship there must also be an acceptance of feelings, both one's own and one's partner's. If one partner doesn't permit the other to be open, that partner places himself or herself in an untenable psychological position. One cannot reject openness and have love. A loving relationship is also a matter of need fulfillment with each partner striving to fulfill the other—a complementary relationship in which roles continually shift from taker to giver. And the openness and need fulfillment depend upon effective listening.

It has been said in jest that before marriage she listens to him and after marriage he listens to her. Unfortunately there often comes a time when neither listens to the other. Openness ceases and the partners no longer meet each other's needs. The marriage dies because love has died.

Abraham Maslow describes the "self-actualized" human as one who has satisfied a number of lower level needs. There are, in Maslow's theory, five levels of needs arranged in hierarchical order. Each lower level of the order must be satisfied at least relatively well before the individual can operate on the next level. The order proceeds from the basic physiological needs of hunger, sex, thirst, sleep, relaxation, and bodily integrity. Next come the "safety" needs which concern the necessity for a world which is orderly and predictable. The world must be just, consistent, safe, and reliable. If these needs are not met, one will feel mistrustful and insecure, restricting his activities to areas of his life he can trust to some degree.

After the safety needs come the needs to share affectionately with others and to belong to a social group. Adequate functioning on this level is evidenced by warm, friendly relationships. This third level involves needs that Maslow calls "love" and "belongingness." Level four needs are the "esteem" needs and include the desire to be important, to achieve, to be independent, and to be free. Also in this group is the need to be competent. Only when the first four levels have been met does the individual reach the level of self-actualization where he is free to utilize the full range of his potentialities, talents, and capacities. And among the self-actualized person's capacities is the capacity to listen.

In his studies of self-actualized people such as Beethoven, Thoreau, Einstein, and Eleanor Roosevelt, Maslow found that they shared a number of personality characteristics. One of those characteristics was the acceptance of themselves and others for what they are. Those who have met or known such people report that when one spoke to them, they listened as though no one else on earth existed at that moment.[2]

Carl Rogers has developed a theory of personality based on his own experiences as a therapist. Rogers found that a process of psychological change occurred in his clients when the clients perceived that he had an "unconditional positive regard" for them. Also included in Rogers' therapeutic process is an empathic understanding of the client's frame of reference. We have referred to this as "knowing where the client is coming from." Because of the therapist's acceptance and understanding, the client becomes increasingly able to talk about his problems and feelings, thus becoming more aware of his alternatives for change. The aim is to make the client's self-concept congruent with his experiences. Complete congruence is evidenced by openness to experience, complete self-acceptance, absence of defensiveness, and effective interpersonal relationships. Rogers' technique was called "nondirective therapy" because unlike other therapists, Rogers did not tell his client how to solve his problem. By listening and encouraging the client to talk, he enabled the client to discover alternatives for himself.[3]

During the decade following Rogers' first book, he began to view the process of therapy as only one kind of interpersonal relationship. He became closely connected with the movement known as "humanistic psychology" and wrote a number of papers explaining his new theory. These were included in his second book, published in 1961.[4]

In Rogers' later revision of his theory the individual's

total experience constitutes his "phenomenal field." The phenomenal field can be known only to the person himself. As the individual develops, part of the phenomenal field gradually becomes differentiated, and this differentiated portion becomes the "self": an organized and consistent whole. The self comprises the individual's perception of his relationships with others, and it seeks actualization by meeting a variety of needs.[5]

These are only two of many theories of personality. One reason I present them is to illustrate the importance of listening and need fulfillment to individual functioning and interpersonal relationships, as visualized in the new humanistic approaches to psychology. A second reason for presenting them is the fact that most of us are not (in Maslow's terms) self-actualized nor are we (in Rogers' terms) persons who are in the process of becoming. Since we are not, we seek to meet our lower level needs. Preoccupied with meeting those needs, we are unable to attend to the needs of others. We are, in short, not free to listen.

While researching an assignment for a magazine, I visited a school in San Diego, California, where perhaps for the first time I saw a program truly designed to meet the needs of children. There were no rows of desks; in fact no desks, as such. Silence was not mandatory, and children were free to wander about the room in search of prearranged learning or activity areas which interested them. No bells rang to signal the opening of school, and in many classrooms groups of adults (teachers and volunteers) and children were already involved in the business of education—learning—even before the scheduled class time. At recess many children literally had to be coaxed outdoors.

That was an amazing and refreshing contrast to the typical situation in which it is apparent that the children attend school to meet the needs of administrators and teachers. What made the San Diego school possible was a unanimous agreement from the superintendent of the district down to the principal of the school that this new approach would be tried. Pressure was taken off the teacher. He or she didn't have to be concerned with an unsatisfactory evaluation because desks were not neatly arranged or children were talking or moving about the room. The teachers' needs on level four of Maslow's hierarchy being met, they were truly able to listen to their pupils and assist them in meeting the needs which school is intended to satisfy.

†The major purpose of this book is to help you develop the skill of listening. By listening, I mean total listening. The total listener is one who listens from the speaker's frame of reference and listens with empathy. This capacity requires that he do two things: first, he must be aware of his own feelings; and second, he must not fear revealing them if they will enhance his interrelationships and his freedom to listen.

Let's turn now to an examination of the sharing of feelings as it relates to the listening process. First of all, what is meant by "the listening process"?

Taylor Caldwell tells the story of John Godfrey. Godfrey was almost an anonymous figure in the town he lived in, but he began a project which would change that. He summoned architects and commissioned them to design and build an odd structure on the land where his home had stood for many years. The architects were puzzled as to why Godfrey wanted such an unusual building, but no less so than the townspeople watching the construction.

Gradually it took shape, a square building faced with marble. A memorial? Maybe a church, some speculated. Once the building itself was completed, the landscaping took form. Beautiful gardens divided by paths of red gravel surrounded the building. Inside were only two rooms. Huge bronze doors provided access. On them were inscribed in gold letters the words "The Man Who Listens." Godfrey's gift to the townspeople was a building where they could always find someone to listen.

In an anteroom visitors sat and waited their turn to

proceed to the inner chamber through an oaken door. Once inside, they found a solitary chair facing an arched alcove curtained with a blue drapery. Alongside the alcove were the words "If you wish to see the man who has listened to you, touch the button above. You will see his face. He will be glad if you thank him, but it is not necessary."

Why did John Godfrey make this unusual building and its listening service available? He explained, "One of the most terrible aspects of this world today is that nobody listens to anyone else. If you are sick, or even dying, nobody listens. If you are bewildered, or frightened, or lost, or bereaved, or alone, or lonely—nobody listens. Even the clergy are hurried and harassed; they do their best and work endlessly. But time has taken on a fragmented character; it doesn't seem to have any substance any longer. Nobody has time to listen to anyone, not even those who love you and would die for you. Your parents, your children, your friends: they have not the time. That's a terrible thing, isn't it? Whose fault is it? I don't know, but there doesn't seem to be any time."

The provision of a constantly available listener by John Godfrey serves as setting for the remainder of Taylor Caldwell's book. Through the bronze doors passes a procession of people with problems. The listener never so much as utters an "uh huh," but remains silent. And yet, just talking helps each character come to a fuller understanding of his problem and discover a direction in which to proceed.[6]

While Caldwell's premise produced a highly interesting story, it is unlikely that Godfrey's idea could provide real solutions to problems. Nevertheless, it does hit at a truth: a problem well-stated is half-solved, and it's the listener who makes this possible.

No doubt someone has said to you, "I have an idea. Listen and let me know what you think." Actually it is not your opinion that was sought by the speaker but your listening ear. In the process of writing a paper or an article, I have often asked my wife or a colleague to listen as I expressed my thoughts or read what I had written. Just hearing myself helped to clarify my ideas. But those were not problems, and I doubt that the mere expressing of problems to another is a totally satisfactory means of solving them. Some sort of feedback is needed which will serve to clarify the feelings behind the expression. The question is, what kind of feedback?

Sidney Jourard suggests that today we know enough about what the healthy personality should be like and the kinds of behavior which enhance mental health to program a course in therapy. Jourard presents the possibility that, reminiscent of Orwell's *1984*, the therapist might respond with a flashing light, a smile, or a glance whenever the patient exhibits a health-promoting behavior. If, as we assume, these responses are reinforcing, the patient will increase the rate of health-promoting behaviors and gradually extinguish those behaviors which produced his symptoms because the latter behaviors are not reinforced.[7]

To carry this idea one step further, biofeedback machines which emit a signal in response to heartbeat, respiration, and blood pressure might well be used in the same manner to provide automatic therapy, with the patient monitoring his own thoughts to prevent—or cause—the signal.

Jourard proposes an automatic therapy machine on which a light is mounted. The patient talks to the machine. If his conversation is bereft of emotional content, the light remains off. But if the patient enters areas of meaningful emotional content, the light, which is connected to his autonomic nervous system, comes on.[8]

Such a procedure cannot produce a healthy personality because, on the one hand, it is a manipulation; and on the other, as Jourard points out, is the fact that not only those considered to have disordered personalities, but those considered "normal" as well, are unable to achieve satisfactory interpersonal relationships. They relate imper-

sonally to others and to themselves. No machine or manipulative psychotherapist can correct that.

It appears, then, that some kind of feedback is necessary when one speaks, and that the feedback must be more
than mechanical. It is not feedback per se which is productive of a healthy personality; it is the interpersonal relationship within which the feedback is couched. But feedback
and interpersonal relationship are obviously inseparable
ingredients, and one cannot determine which comes first.
So let's look first at the kind of relationship which is necessary to proper feedback, and then at the quality of the
feedback itself and how and why it is an agent for change.

I spoke earlier of the need for openness. When listening to someone, the assumption is that unlike John Godfrey, you will make some kind of reply. The usefulness of
your reply will depend to a great extent on your willingness to share your feelings. For example, a friend on the
verge of tears tells you, "My boyfriend just told me he
wanted to call it quits, and I just don't know what to do.
I can't stand the thought of losing him." What do you say?
If you can acknowledge your own feelings, you will make
one kind of response. If you are fearful of letting your
friend know how deeply you feel about her problem or of
admitting it to yourself, or if you're unaware of what your
feeling is, you will make quite another.

Sidney Jourard feels that most of us hide our real
selves in our transactions with others; that we relate im-
personally not only to others but to ourselves as well. Because we role-play in accordance with the self which we
identify with, the real self is not permitted to emerge if it
is inconsistent with either the roles we play or with our
self-concept.[9]

An excellent example of this was provided by a co-
worker who once said during one of my communication
workshops, "Anyone who lets down his defenses these days
is crazy." I knew this person not by his words but by his
actions, which were completely inconsistent with the self

he presented in public. Others saw him as being crotchety, unfriendly, and inconsiderate. In actual fact he was the kind of person who would do anything he could to help, would go out of his way to perform a favor. Moreover, he had an excellent sense of humor. It was obvious that he was constantly under stress to keep from revealing his true self. Walking about with a sour face when one actually wishes to smile can become very wearing. But his role was that of "sourpuss."

Only when one is permitted to talk about oneself without fear of censure can one speak freely. This is what occurs in therapy. At first the patient's statements are defensive and designed to make the therapist think well of him. In a sense he says what he thinks the therapist wants to hear. I encounter this phenomenon frequently when I work with families. At the outset, despite the fact that we are together because the family is coming apart at the seams, they present a united front to convince me and each other that all is well. Gradually, as it becomes clear that I am not judge and jury and that I deal with the family as though I were a member of it, they open up—not just to me, but to each other. For the first time they're able to say things to one another they never thought they could, and they're able to accept what is said.

Speaking of the effect of therapy on the individual, Jourard says that as the patient goes through the treatment process, he comes to understand more of his motives, wishes, and feelings than ever before. Frequently he becomes more spontaneous in his behavior with others, and his friends notice the change in his willingness to acknowledge a broader range of motives. The experience has apparently changed his behavior pattern from responses which caused and perpetuated his symptoms to patterns which produce more positive and acceptable results. Jourard describes the process as

the experience of being permitted to be—to be himself, the experience of being utterly attended to by a professional man who is of goodwill, who seeks to understand him utterly and to communicate both his goodwill and his understanding *as these grow*. It is the experience of feeling free to be and to disclose himself in the presence of another human person whose goodwill is assured, but whose responses are unpredictable. . . . It is the manner of the therapist's *being* when in the presence of the patient. *Effective* therapists seem to follow this implicit hypothesis: If they are *themselves* in the presence of the patient, if they let their patient and themselves be, avoiding *compulsions* to silence, to reflection, to interpretation, to impersonal technique, and kindred character disorders, but instead striving to know their patient, involving themselves in his situation, and then responding to his utterances with their spontaneous selves, this fosters growth. In short, they love their patients.[10]

The concept of spontaneity and being oneself was expressed more than twenty-five hundred years ago in the words of Chinese philosopher Lao-Tse, founder of Taoism: "The way to do is to be."

Having decided to accept your own feelings in relationships with others—to "own" them, as it were—you will find that you no longer need to worry about their getting in the way. If what the speaker says makes you sad, you can deal with that sadness. If he makes you angry, you can deal with that too. The point is that you couldn't hide those feelings in any case. They would surface whether you wanted them to or not—if not verbally, then nonverbally. A raised eyebrow, a change in body position, a clenched fist, a shrugged shoulder, a wistful look, any of these could give you away. But they are not the kinds of feedback which will cause the speaker to clarify his position and enable you to maintain a healthy relationship.

McMahon and Campbell write, "We do not come to believe in ourselves until someone reveals that deep inside us something is valuable, worth listening to, worthy of our trust, sacred to our touch. Once we believe in ourselves we can risk curiosity . . . wonder . . . spontaneous delight or any experience that reveals the human spirit."[11]

We sometimes use the term "confirmation of the other." As stated by Martin Buber, the term implies more than affirmation or acceptance; more, even, than empathy. Confirming another means that we imagine in a concrete way what the other person is wishing, feeling, thinking, and perceiving at the moment. It involves quite literally, as Buber says, "a swinging into the other which demands the intensest action of one's being." True confirmation requires that one person confirm another as *being* this existing being even though he opposes him.

On the matter of self-disclosure, Buber in his concept "I and Thou" makes a distinction between what he calls the "primary word I-It" which conveys the experience and action occurring *within* the person; and the "primary word I-Thou" which takes place *between* the person and the world. Problems of relationship occur in this area of the *between*.

As Buber says, "The essential problematic of the sphere of the between is the duality of being and seeming. The man dominated by being gives himself to the other without thinking about the image of himself awakened in the beholder. The seeming man, in contrast, is primarily concerned with what the other thinks of him and produces a look calculated to make himself appear spontaneous, sincere, or whatever he thinks will win the other's approval. This 'seeming' destroys the authenticity of the life between man and man and thus the authenticity of human existence in general. The tendency toward seeming originates in man's need for confirmation and his desire to be confirmed falsely rather than not be confirmed at all."[12]

With the admonition to "be that self one truly is" should also come a word of caution. There needs to be a governor on self-disclosure. I have seen the results of ill-run encounter (and other kinds of therapy) groups. The worst example was produced by a Transactional Analysis group. I witnessed a reasonably pleasant personality change almost overnight into one that was obnoxiously aggressive and overbearing. This person thought that the key to becoming a healthy personality was complete openness. The result was that he began to tell each person he met precisely how in his opinion they were "not O.K."

One day I saw this person berating another and decided to ask him about his experiences in the Transactional Analysis group. I pointed out that whereas the aim of the group was to arrive at a point where the members would have an "I'm O.K.—You're O.K." attitude, he appeared to be at the "I'm O.K.—You're *not* O.K." stage. He replied that his understanding was that the "O.K. person" was able to express his feelings and that's what he was doing. "That's real communication," he pointed out, "and if the group didn't do anything else, it did teach me to recognize and express my feelings. It's good for people to know where they need to improve."

It's true of course that the ability to be aware of and to express one's feelings and thoughts is valuable. But at the same time, one has an obligation to act responsibly in so doing. In a dialogue with another it isn't necessary, unless it is relevant to the dialogue, to disclose all your feelings about him or your situation with him. If one is asked, one may still reserve the right to judge whether it would be helpful to the asker and to oneself to disclose one's feeling. But one must reveal one's judgment not to disclose, if that is one's decision. By the same token, if one is asked to make a self-disclosure, one has the right to privacy.

Dr. Jourard tells of being invited to address a group at Esalen Institute in California. His subject was to be his book *The Transparent Self* and anything else germane. During his presentation he was frequently interrupted with complaints that he was talking *about* self-disclosure but not practicing it. Finally exasperated by one person in particular, he said, "Damn it! You're not asking for self-disclosure, which I'm doing! You seem to want a strip tease! Would you like me to undress? Look, if you want to sit with me and talk, I'm ready. But I'm a private person. Respect this as much as I respect your right to disclose or withhold."[13]

Buber, on the same subject, said, "Communication does not depend on one saying to another everything that occurs to him—on letting one's self go—only on letting no 'seeming' creep in between him and the other."[14]

It is not only unnecessary to share all of one's feelings at all times; it can damage one's interpersonal relationships to do so. My friend from the Transactional Analysis group soon found this to be true.

This chapter has concerned the idea of self-disclosure, but now we want to use that idea in relation to the other side of the coin—listening. Earlier in this chapter it was stated that our task is to get the other person to talk freely about his feelings—to get him to let us into his world. That requires recognition and acceptance of the other's feelings. But in order to succeed at that, we must be able to recognize our own feelings and be aware of them. We cannot come to know ourselves except as an outgrowth of disclosing ourselves to another—in the process of helping the other disclose himself. It is in the process of helping the other disclose himself to himself that we come to understand him—and ourselves.

What has been called the "dialogue" between two people does not consist in a mere reflection of what another says, but in seeking confirmation that what the listener understood the speaker to say is what he intended to say. More than that, it is permitting the speaker to say what he intended, whether or not the listener agrees.

Part II of this book will deal with the roots of schizophrenic listening. In chapter 5 we will look at the way in which listening patterns are shaped during one's earliest months and years by the family and home environment. But before we proceed, I will ask you to complete one more exercise.

On a sheet of paper, first jot down as many of your feelings as you are aware of at this moment. Use the left side of the page for a one-word description of your feelings right now. Take a minute to do this. Then, in the right-hand column, list as many feelings (including those in the first column) as you can think of. My experience with this exercise tells me that another minute will be sufficient for most of us. Begin now, and when the two minutes have expired or when you have run out of feelings to jot down, read on.

No, you needn't save this list. The idea was to illustrate how few feelings we can identify and how pitifully unaware of our own feelings most of us are at any given moment. In part III we will work on expanding your awareness of your feelings so that you can recognize and deal with them. Only then will you be able to be aware of others' expressions of feelings.

Part II

Home, Family, School: Reality Starts Here

The reason you don't understand me,
Edith, is because I'm talkin' to you in
English and you're listenin' in dingbat!

Archie Bunker

5

Suffer
the Little Children

When I was "growing up" several decades ago, part
of the parental credo was that children were to be "seen
and not heard." We were frequently given the word by our
parents but admonished against using it. Things are certainly different today. At least in many homes children *are*
being heard. Unfortunately the word they are given frequently comes from sources outside the home and is usually limited to four letters. What's more, admonitions
against using the word are lacking in force because often
Mom and Dad also use it.

I'm not going to preach about profanity and obscenity.
What becomes of the American language will happen despite any effort I might make to change the course of
events. I accept the fact that my language is what it is; I
accept whatever yours is. But I think we should both be
aware that it isn't what language we use that's important,
but how well we use our language to say what we want.

Mark Twain's wife, Olivia, found the profanity he
used so frequently in his lectures offensive. One evening
as she helped him with his necktie before a lecture, she at-

tempted a tactic to stop him from using such language. She uttered a lengthy string of his favorite words. Twain just looked at her and smiled.

"Libby," he said. "You've got the words, but you ain't got the music."

The music is the important thing, not the words. As Jess Lair put it, there's no such thing as correctness of language. "That fear screws up all the things we say.... This language is a living thing, and the way you and I use it is the way she is."[1] The trouble with the kind of parental emphasis on language that I and many other children my age experienced is that it was more concerned with the selection of words than with their appropriateness to the feelings to be described; more concerned with the proper sequencing of words than with their communicative value.

I want to discuss the possibilities for personal growth inherent in the relationships we have with our parents during the preschool years. I would like you to decide whether the process by which you came to be you was one of introjection or one of projection. Are you really who your parents told you you are? Or are you actually holding on to that belief as a means of preserving your self-esteem?

Perls believes that we project our consciences onto our parents. They were too strict or too easy, too affectionate or cold, and so on. But as long as we continue to lay our problems at our parents' doorstep we continue to ask to be judged by them, to seek their approval. We continue to exist *as them* rather than as ourselves.[2] We are we because they are they.

An unknown author wrote the following explanation of the origins of adult behavior:

CHILDREN LEARN WHAT THEY LIVE

If a child lives with criticism, he learns to condemn.
If a child lives with acceptance, he learns to love.
If a child lives with hostility, he learns to fight.
If a child lives with approval, he learns to like himself.

If a child lives with fear, he learns to be apprehensive.
If a child lives with recognition, he learns to have a goal.
If a child lives with pity, he learns to be sorry for himself.
If a child lives with fairness, he learns what justice is.
If a child lives with jealousy, he learns to feel guilty.
If a child lives with honesty, he learns what truth is.
If a child lives with encouragement,
*   he learns to be confident.*
If a child lives with tolerance,
*   he learns to be patient.*
If a child lives with praise,
*   he learns to be appreciative.*
If a child lives with security,
*   he learns to have faith in himself.*
If a child lives with friendliness,
*   he learns that a world is the nice place to live.*

A student told me, "I read that list, and I can trace some of what I am. I can still remember my father's invariable reaction when I brought home an infrequent good grade from school. If I got ninety-nine points on a test, he would look at the paper carefully—examining, I suppose, the one mistake—and then ask, 'What happened to the other point?' I don't know how I responded to that kind of reaction to my efforts at first, but after awhile I said nothing. In that exchange when I play it back now, there's no stated criticism—maybe my father was trying to show me that he had confidence in me and knew I could get that other point. Or maybe I never understood his sense of humor."

That young man had been trained by example to believe that only his father's words were carrying the message. Apparently neither of them knew how to listen to the other. If the father's feeling was one of humor, he didn't communicate it and his son didn't see it. If the son's feeling was one of hurt, he didn't communicate that either, and his father didn't see it.

The student continued, "I took that question 'What

happened to the other point, or two points, or five points?'
as criticism of me. I'm a perfectionist, and in part, at least,
I attribute my perfectionistic obsession with that experience. I lived with it for years, and I argued vehemently
with anyone who told me that I was a perfectionist."

That happened to be one of my traits, too, and I disclosed that to him.

"You know" I said, "It was my inability to think that
anyone else could do things as well as I that finally did me
in, yet at the same time showed me the way out. After a
certain period of time in just about any professional field,
I expect that it's normal to require the services of a secretary. I have two. My wife, Margaret, helps me with researching, types all of my manuscripts, takes care of all the
bookkeeping, and so she's my secretary when I'm wearing
my writer's hat. It's a fairly recent endeavor which she resigned from teaching to accept—at no pay.

"Jean is my secretary when I'm wearing my psychologist's hat. Like my wife, Jean does more things to make my
work easier than I could possibly tell you. One of the best
things those ladies did for me was make me come to grips
with my perfectionism.

"I began to notice that my work load as a psychologist increased in volume when I had a secretary. I wondered why that should be. I told myself I'd be better off
without a secretary. I could just farm out the typing; I
transcribed all my reports anyway. It seemed as though I
spent more time telling Jean how to do things than it
would take me to do them myself.

"At about the same time I was being inundated by details of setting up some workshop groups, my writing work
load also mushroomed. I turned over everything I could to
my wife, which saved much of my time and effort in the
writing department. That wasn't easy for me to do—I had
a great need to retain instant-by-instant control—but I
forced myself to let go, still not admitting to myself that
I was perfectionistic. What I had to learn was that con-

stantly striving to control has the opposite effect. One becomes controlled.

"My secretary, Jean, is an excellent psychologist as well as an excellent secretary. When I told her all the responsibility I had given my wife, she said in her soft Texas manner, 'You know, even though your wife isn't a trained secretary, she can save you so much work. All you have to do is be willing to accept some mistakes. They can always be corrected.'

"Immediately it hit me. The reason my work seemed to increase when Jean became my part-time secretary was because I was doing everything twice: once for myself and once to show her exactly how to do *her* job. After that I began to turn over a lot of detail work and some of my responsibilities to Jean, and I began to get compliments about how much better I was running things and taking care of details. I began to see that I was not as perfect as I tried to convince myself I was. She not only did things as well as I did, but did many of them better."

A man who is bilingual may be worth two people, but with two capable secretaries I found that a man can do three jobs. And he can learn a lesson. Now that's a heartwarming story, but don't assume that having someone make you realize that you have some trait that you'd rather not have will rid you of it. If you get anything from Carl Rogers, get this: the understanding that you can't force a change in yourself. What I've done is to accept the fact that I'm a perfectionist. I'm not trying to change that, but simply by being aware of it I can see that the trait acquired during my first years of living is very gradually evaporating. I probably won't live long enough to see it disappear, but it won't be a problem.

That kind of self-awareness and self-understanding can happen only when that openness and sharing I talked about in chapter 4 exists. Only when you understand another and he understands you can you be aware of who you are and where you're coming from at any given point in

time. You may be committed to the psychoanalytic view
that your inabilities are the result of childhood traumas.
Maybe you agree with Perls that those so-called traumas
are actually projections onto your parents. The important
thing is that when your pattern of interpersonal relationships was being cut, the area of the between, the *Mitwelt*,
either was or was not entered—or perhaps was not entered
when it should have been. Let's turn to the question of
why this happens.

It was noted that the opinion "children should be seen
and not heard" was given wide credence a few years ago.
My experience is that this doctrine still has some pretty
loyal adherents. One of them was a father whose unhappy
wife came to see me with their eight-year-old daughter in
tow. Her husband had insisted that he and she take their
evening meals on a tray in the living room while their
daughter ate in the kitchen by herself.

"Why does he insist on that?" I asked.

"He says he can't stand Jenny's talking at the table.
He comes home tired and wants to sit and read the paper
and then eat his dinner without any disturbance."

"Disturbance?"

"He says that Jenny's talking disturbs him."

"What does Jenny talk about, and whom does she talk
to?"

"Oh, she tells us about what she did in school, maybe
a story she read. You know, the kinds of things kids usually talk about."

"Does he ever talk with her?"

"He says that there's a time and a place for kids to
talk, and dinnertime is not the time or place."

"What is the time and place?"

"There isn't one, I guess."

Well, that's enough to give you an idea of the problem
and the direction that counseling might take; and it also
indicates that the old notion of silent kids is still alive and
well. That's just one example of many similar ones I've en-

countered, but in every such case there's the same absence of sharing. And to add to that list of "Children Learn What They Live": If a child lives in a world of deaf ears and insensitivity to needs, he learns to be a schizophrenic listener.

Most of the trouble we have in producing good listeners stems from our child-rearing practices; but not all of it originates from not listening or not providing good models. Other factors may be lacking. Listening isn't the only kind of attention that kids need. Another kind is at least as important.

Jess Lair tells about the way Zulu parents—the entire Zulu community, in fact—raise their children. Zulu children are "nursed at their mother's breast, and carried on [their] mother's back with [their] bare skin against her warm, bare skin for two solid years."[3]

That kind of physical contact is more than most children in this country receive from their parents throughout their entire lives. When the Zulu child's two years of carriage were over and his mother had a new baby, he entered an extended family that included his entire village. If he didn't have older brothers or sisters, another child of the village would pick him up and hold him if he cried or just wanted to be held; or one of the adults, man or woman, would carry him until he stopped crying. Because there was so much love received by all the villagers, there was a lot of love available for giving.

In addition to receiving an ample supply of love, the Zulu is also taught to accept himself. An example is found in the custom of the elders to tell each of the girls "you are very beautiful. You are very beautiful because you were uniquely created by our God. You are an Aleluthi. And everyone knows that all the children in the Aleluthi family have always been very beautiful."[4]

Now those are two pretty nice inheritances—an abundance of love to share and self-acceptance of one's physical being. Beauty inside and out. How many of us in this enlightened culture had all the love we wanted as children? How many of us were certain that we were beautiful? I've found that most parents don't even realize what qualities are lacking in their children's lives that are needed for their psychological growth.

As the nation's economic conditions worsen, parents are concerned with financial survival. The quality of nurturance in the home suffers, and all sorts of devices are employed to conceal the deterioration. "Many families that look fine on the outside turn out to be soft, or even rotten on the inside," according to psychiatrist Nathan Ackerman, a noted marriage and family counselor.[5]

According to writer Richard Gehman, a new order of discipline is needed. He points out that many experts have blamed the poor condition of family life on a lack of discipline. For example, Dr. Benjamin Spock, whose famous "Baby Book" guided the rearing of a generation of children, has warned of the lack of leadership in the home. "Parents," says Dr. Spock, "seem to be forgetting some of their responsibility to be strong and directive with children."[6]

In his recent book Spock repeats this warning. He says it's not a question of leniency, but rather what is behind the method. Often parents give an outward show of strictness, but there's no substance to what they pretend so the child takes over. Firm leadership is what's needed.[7] The need for limit-setting has been stressed over the past few years by other specialists such as psychologists Haim Ginott and Fitzhugh Dodson.

Another reason frequently given for the deteriorating condition of the family is the rapid change in values. Increased mobility, a glut of consumer goods, more efficient and varied means of communication, and the demands of ethnic minorities for equal shares of life—all have eaten away at traditional values. The bonds of family life seem loosened, and the home's influence on children appears weakened.

Gehman cites Dr. Harold A. Edgerton of Performance Research, Inc., a nonprofit corporation engaged in psychological research, as placing responsibility for lack of parental direction on these changes in environmental conditions. Parental expectations, Dr. Edgerton feels, can no longer be what they were two generations ago.[8]

A counselor acquaintance recently pointed out that reward and punishment are no longer useful approaches to child-rearing because they imply that the person who does the rewarding or punishing is superior. Perls describes this relationship: "The topdog usually is righteous and authoritarian; he knows best. He is sometimes right, but always righteous. The topdog is a bully, and works with 'You should' and 'You should not.' The topdog manipulates with demands and threats of catastrophe, such as, 'If you don't, then—you won't be loved, you won't go to heaven, you will die,' and so on."[9]

The need is for parents and children to reason together, for parents to talk with, not to, their children. This is an idea proposed by Dr. Rudolph Dreikurs, who suggested a "family council" to settle crises.[10]

At the same time that the experts were debating whether parents or changing times had caused the breakdown in family life and how it could be corrected, parents themselves were developing a repertoire of games to get themselves off the hook.

There is, for example, the EVERYTHING I'M DOING IS FOR THEM game. When I recently advised a father to spend more time with his son, he replied that his efforts to earn enough to provide well for his family took most of his free time as well as his working hours, but that he would try to schedule an hour each Sunday morning. As deplorable as that game may seem, at least the father was honest enough to state his priorities; and in that respect perhaps he's a notch above many other parents. Many are either too dishonest to admit, or too unaware to recognize, that their families are in trouble.

A much used cover-up is the game called I'VE GOT MINE, NOW YOU GET YOURS. This involves engaging in a frenzy of supposedly "family activities" in which the parents hope to give the illusion that their family is a functioning, healthy organization. Such families actually consist of strangers living solitary, parallel lives in the same house. Each parent serves his or her own needs rather than those of the children or one another. A few days ago I heard a father who managed a Little League team tell his son, "It wasn't my team's fault they lost the game last night—winning or losing is *my* responsibility." Since he doesn't manage his son's team, go to any of his son's games, or show any interest in them, it would seem that he's involved in Little League for reasons more closely related to his own needs than to his son's. And I could point to several mothers who are so involved in PTA activities that they have no time for their own children!

Another smoke screen frequently employed to hide poor family functioning is the TEN LITTLE INDIANS game. The family that prays together may stay together, but they won't really want to unless there is genuine togetherness. Some parents I've seen have artificially involved themselves with their children to such an extent that they have become social dropouts. "We never leave the children out of our plans," they tell you, but they're more motivated by the desire to be able to say that than by any real enjoyment in being with their offspring. Such involvements are contrived, insincere, and divisive in their effects. Soon one parent or the other begins to make excuses to get out of family activities; then, one by one, the children follow suit until all are going their separate ways.

Equally futile is the thought that parents can hold the family together by loosening restrictions—the ANYTHING TO KEEP PEACE IN THE FAMILY game. One of the most insecure, frightened, demanding, and unloving children I have ever met in therapy came from a home where almost no rules applied. He told me, "My parents don't love me; they don't care what I do." His mother told me. "His father gets so annoyed at the boy's nagging that he tells me to let him do whatever he's pestering for if it will shut him up."

Overindulgence, too, can destroy families. Parents may try to rid themselves of family responsibility, try to avoid emotional involvement by providing the children and each other with material things. This game is called I'VE GIVEN YOU ALL THE LOVE MONEY CAN BUY. The husband, for example, may shower his wife with gifts. In other forms of this game self-love is involved, and either spouse may be affected. The characteristic is overindulgence—in alcohol, one's career, whatever—extramarital affairs are symptomatic, too.

Another family preservation game is the one I call PUTTING THE BLAME ON MAME. It employs an overt attempt to show that everything would be all right with the family if it weren't for one particular member. When families are referred to me for counseling, I find what family therapist Virginia Satir has called the "Identified Patient," or IP—the individual whom the rest of the family says it would be all right "if it weren't for. . . ." Most often, in my experience, that individual is one of the children.[11] We find that the Identified Patient is really a symptom of what's ailing the family. As long as the IP remains "ill," the family can continue to function. It's not surprising that such families resist therapy, often unconsciously. They miss appointments, forget to return phone calls, or claim that they just don't care for the therapist. So the IP doesn't get well, the balance within the family is not disturbed, and the family remains unhealthy but intact.

Then there's the STICK WITH ME, KID game. Some mothers and fathers use children as pawns in a kind of parental chess match. The idea is to maintain what they presume to be control over the children. They try to persuade their children to side with one or the other of them in disputes. An alternative is for one parent to side with the children against the other parent. In either case, when the children sense the weakness in their parents and the lack of a strong, unified disciplinary program, they are uneasy with the vacuum. In order to fill it, they assume control of the home. And children tend to be tyrannical rulers.

Why do parents play these games? I believe it's because they've bought the idea that their values are outdated. It's the easy way out. For one thing, they're preoccupied with the problem of financial survival at a time when social status and the number of machines and gadgets one owns are synonymous. So it's easier for them to accept the idea that changing times have forced them to discard old values than to try holding on to them. It's also easier to pretend that this is what the children want—a new freedom for new times.

But do young people really want their parents to discard these old values? Is family life no longer important to them? Students in fifteen high schools in Sweden, supposedly a country at the leading edge of the new wave of freedom, indicate otherwise. In a report of the Psychology of Religion Institute, Dr. Berndt Gustafsson says that for these twelve hundred students "a pleasant home milieu comes very high on the list of wishes for the future, together with marriage and sexual satisfaction." A similar study at the University of Texas shows that "Texas youth are and have been assimilating the value systems of their parents into their own to a greater extent then the public generally assumes." This conclusion was based on replies of some eight hundred senior students to a questionnaire distributed at the University's Austin campus.[12]

As for taking control of the home, young people don't want that either. I recently interviewed children in four schools on the subject of discipline. The great majority (73 percent) felt that teachers and parents should be more strict. "I don't want my dad to be like a Marine drill sergeant," one junior high school student said, "but I'd sure feel a lot better if I knew what he expected of me."

If the family is to survive as an institution, it must be

sufficiently flexible to adopt and adapt to worthwhile changes in values as well as hold on to those traditional values which have served well in the past. Children and young people, just as adults, want security, a home base they can rely on. Without the feeling that the world is a safe place we don't have the freedom to be ourselves. Values which serve well will prevail in the long run if children have their way.

A good example is seen in man's relationship to his world which, as it changes, becomes more the same. Look at the "back to nature" trend. Although today's youth think that they have discovered something new, they have really turned backward. I recall hearing philosopher Eric Hoffer remark that man shows his civilization by moving away from nature. My generation was in accord with that philosophy, and perhaps we moved too far from nature too fast. The younger generation is moving us back and preserving the best of a worthwhile tradition. They will also preserve the family if they are given a bit of help; and in the process I believe they will show us the way toward greater openness and sharing. But to help them do this we must remember what it was like to be young. That idea has been incorporated into the training of marriage and family counselors.

An introductory exercise used at the Family Therapy Institute of Marin is helpful not only to student therapists but possibly to all of us. People who go through this program at San Raphael, California, begin their training by becoming children. That may sound a bit strange, but it really makes sense to start a study of the family with a better understanding of what it's like to be a child. In order to understand what it's like to be a child, you have to travel that way yourself once in awhile. How many of us really recall how it was when we were children; the times we anguished over a poor report card; the fear we had that when Mommy and Daddy went out for the evening they might never come back; the panic at being abandoned, perhaps, on your first day in kindergarten; the terror of a loud argument between Mom and Dad? If we could remember our feelings at such times, we would certainly relate to our own children and to each other with greater empathy and understanding of what makes us and our families tick.

Without children, there wouldn't be a family. They are often the determining factor in important parental decisions. Frequently, as I've said, they are used as pawns in a parental chess game. Often they are the "glue" that holds marriages and families together, and unfortunately it's usually one of the children who is the major victim when the family fails.

The main objective of this introductory program at the Family Therapy Institute is diagnosis. Although it might disavow the "medical model," I will take the liberty of likening the need for diagnosis of the family—the roles assigned or assumed by the members, the rules which govern intrafamily behaviors, etc.—to the need for diagnosis in disease: Until the physician knows what the illness is, he can't do a very effective job of curing it. In the case of the Family Therapy Institute, the diagnosis begins with an examination of the varying roles of children.

So the idea of having student counselors become children is practical. The trainees are instructed to divide into four groups. Those in the first group are told to pretend they are all only-children; those in the second, that they are oldest children; the third group consists of middle children; and the fourth, youngest children. Each group discusses what its own experience is like, how each person sees his role as an only, oldest, middle, or youngest child and what his feelings are.

Here are reactions from the members of one class who went through the experience. Check them against your own idea of what it was like for you as a child, how it is for you now—and, if you have children, how it is for them. Do you see yourself?

Those in the group of only-children reported that they saw themselves as:

1. Being alone; consensus that the only-child feels loneliness.
2. Subject to heavy parental control but generally submissive and adhering closely to established rules.
3. Unable to handle hostilities because they had no siblings to learn to fight with.
4. Somewhat overindulged, their every whim or interest being met almost immediately.
5. Unskilled in sharing because of nobody to share with, and unable to learn through interaction with older siblings.
6. Having a great burden of responsibility to meet unfulfilled parental needs.

The students in the oldest child group had these comments:

1. Three major roles were expected of them: caretakers of the younger children; example-setters for them; and parental trainers—it fell to them to "break in" Mom and Dad as parents.
2. As older children, the most oriented toward superior achievement.
3. Resentful toward the heavy responsibilities placed upon them although they accepted them.
4. More serious than their younger siblings.
5. More independent.

From the youngest child group came these reactions and statements:

1. Assumption of responsibility characterized as "if nobody else will do it, I'll do it."
2. Generally inactive unless and until pressure was exerted.

3. Whatever "injustices" they were—or imagined they were—subjected to, they harbored very little resentment.
4. Agreed that as youngest children they often experienced emotional upset, sometimes severe, so that the family "homeostasis" or balance could be preserved.
5. Would accept little responsibility even under pressure.

The group composed of middle children felt like this:

1. Functioned as go-betweens for family messages and other family members.
2. The Henry Kissingers of the family, serving as mediators in disputes among family members—keepers-of-the-peace.
3. Spent much time observing the process within the family—the give-and-take—and could tell an outsider (e.g., a family counselor) what was happening in the family at any given time.
4. Acted *in loco parentis* with other, younger siblings and tended to baby them.
5. Felt a sense of competition, especially with a sibling of the same sex who was one of two in a row and close to the same age. Much of the competition was concerned with the peacekeeping role.

How did you come out? Did your childhood recollections of your own family agree pretty much with those of the Family Therapy Institute students? Or were they quite a lot different? Maybe you found it difficult to remember how it was for you. In chapter 9 we'll take an in-depth look at how these early home and family influences have shaped your ability to be open about your feelings.

In this chapter I've talked about some of the ways we learn poor listening habits from out parents. First is the unwillingness of many parents even to hear children. Second is the inability to distinguish between hearing and listening. Major factors in the acquisition of poor listening habits include the psychological inadequacies of the home environment. Parents often indulge in game-playing to avoid acknowledging these inadequacies. When there isn't enough openness, love, and acceptance, there's no sharing. Without mutual sharing, child and parents never come to know and understand one another or themselves. Without understanding yourself, you never learn to tune in to your own feelings. You never become able to describe or express your feelings, and so you're unable to help others share their feelings with you.

In chapter 6 we'll take a closer look at parent-child interactions—how they shape self-concept and affect the way we relate to others and how children become game-playing parents.

To let go of the parents, and especially to forgive the parents is the hardest thing for most people to do.   Frederick S. Perls

6

You Made Me What I Am Today

During the life of the Third Reich, horrible things were done; things which we hope will never be forgotten. The almost universal defense of those accused of war crimes following the Nazi defeat was to hide behind authority. They laid the guilt on superiors: "I was only following orders."

The introductory quotation from Perls points up how strong the tendency is for the human animal to blame others for his failures. But we know that "you" didn't make me what I am today. If I am you, then I'm not a person.

We develop our first perceptions of who and what we are, our idea of "self," at our parents' knees. The question of the degree to which heredity or environment determines the self-concept is of little importance. What is important is how the self-concept develops. Now that we've blamed our parents and the world at large for the holes in our personalities, let's begin to zero in on the persons who could have done something about it and didn't: ourselves. How did I, how did you, become the way we are now?

One hypothesis called the "phenomenal theory of personality" is based on the "perceptual field," which is described as "the universe of naive experience in which each individual lives, the everyday situation of the self and its surroundings which each person takes to be reality."[1] In the view of phenomenology, only our own perceptual or phenomenal field is reality; the other person's field is only his own interpretation of reality, not reality itself. My short story "Analog" was a good example of what is meant by this. As the author of that story, only I can explain what it intended to say because it was my reality from which it originated. If your understanding of the story differs from my reality, that is merely your *interpretation* of reality as far as I'm concerned.

Rogers' theory has elements of phenomenology. He believes that two structural components are basic to personality: the "self" and the "organism." The organism is the location of the phenomenal field which is the individual's frame of reference that can be known only to the individual.[2]

In phenomenal theory the self in a given situation is called the "phenomenal self." Among the perceptions of self which together make up the phenomenal self, many have little or no value in describing who and what you are. You may, for example, perceive yourself to be an excellent tennis player; but that perception is of little or no importance in describing your behavior in all situations.

On the other hand, very important perceptions do exist among the thousand which combine to make up your phenomenal self. You perceive yourself as being a woman, for example. That perception helps in predicting your behavior in all situations at all times. Together with other important perceptions from the phenomenal self, the perception that you're a woman is part of your "self-concept."

We must remember that we are not just one isolated part of our phenomenal self or single self-perception. We are an organized whole, and whatever affects any part causes changes in the whole. These changes can cause severe personality disorders. For instance, many men who have had vasectomies later experience dysfunctioning in their sexual performance. They perceived themselves to be males, and as males they also perceived themselves as capable of producing offspring. Following the operation, they may feel they have lost their maleness because they realize that they can no longer fulfill the male function of reproduction. As a result, they may become impotent.

We perceive ourselves to be male, female, likeable or unlikeable, tall or short, beautiful or ugly as a result of the experiences we meet in our environment—especially with other people and, in particular, with our parents and family. As previously noted, the relationships we have with our parents are crucial in forming our personality.

As we develop, we receive continual input from parents and others. Rarely if ever is this input fully consonant with the way we are. We're approved of for some things we do and disapproved of for other things. In order to become self-actualized, we must learn to accept what we are. As Rogers puts it, "What this seems to mean is that the individual comes to *be*—in awareness—what he *is*—in experience. He is, in other words, a complete and fully functioning human organism."[3]

Good or bad, not all interactions with our parents have lasting results. Even if our interactions were healthful ones, personal and social influences can alter them and cause maladjustments. Similarly, interpersonal relations with one's parents which were not productive of a healthy personality can be ameliorated or corrected by personal and societal influences. Some kinds of parent-child interrelationships, however, are rather consistently found in the backgrounds of persons with disturbed personalities. Some of these backgrounds include the following:

Rejection. If a child feels rejected, unloved, and unwanted by his parents, he is likely to develop a negative self-concept. He will probably also lack standards by which

to judge whether particular actions are acceptable or un-
acceptable. Rejecting parents give their children neither
approval nor disapproval, praise nor criticism. Children
whose parents consistently reject them tend to develop
their moral sense slowly. As adults they have a hard time
showing affection for, or accepting it from, others.

Perfectionism. I mentioned earlier the problems I had
with perfectionism. If your parents made perfectionistic
demands on you that you excel in sports or academic
activities, for example, and you had the intelligence and
skill to measure up—you probably came out all right. But
that isn't usually the case, because there seems to be no
satisfying of perfectionistic parents. If you pitched one no-
hitter last season, you'd better count on pitching at least
two this year. If your grade-point average last year was
3.9, you'll be expected to carry more units this year and
still keep that 4-point. Eventually you'll feel frustrated,
and when you see that no matter how hard you try your
best is never good enough, you'll finally say "to hell with
it" and stop trying. Even if you can by some miracle meet
all the demands, the pressure you're under stunts your
psychological growth.

Poor discipline. Firm, consistent discipline is essential.
Countless children became fouled-up adults because their
parents mistook unconditional acceptance for absolute permissiveness; and Dr. Spock, who intended no such thing,
was blamed. Psychologists have known for years that a
high correlation exists between permissiveness and anti-
social behavior. The home in which there is poor discipline
also provides an insecure base for children. If discipline is
too strict, the result may be a fearful person who resents
the disciplining parent and other authority figures. Children whose parents were overly repressive tend toward
rigidity and are self-critical. Inconsistent discipline also
leads to a weak value structure and poor self-discipline.

I was addressing one of my parent groups about the
need to be consistent, to treat a misdeed today the same

way one treated the same misdeed last week and the week before. One of the parents, a young mother with three boys, interrupted to say that she didn't agree with me. She said that she took into consideration how both she and the child felt at the time. "We all have good and bad days," she said. I replied that she was certainly within her rights to handle things that way and asked her what her success rate had been in eliminating problem behaviors. She was honest in admitting that it was "just about zero." I already knew that her youngsters were famous for their misbehaviors at school. It's just as important, of course, to avoid forcing the child into a preconceived mold. To do so causes him to lose his existence as an individual and therefore interferes with his psychological development.

Smotherhood. Another cause of improper personality development is overprotection, or what might be called "smotherhood" or "momism." Overprotective mothers prevent their children from taking risks. At the extreme the children are kept away from other people and even kept in sterile environments so they won't become ill. Frequently because the mother's marital adjustment is poor, contact between mother and child is excessive and seductive. The mother looks upon the child as her lover and actually calls him that.

A psychologist friend told me of a counseling session he had with the mother of a boy about five years old. She arrived for the appointment with the boy in tow and asked if it would be all right if he stayed with her. She didn't trust baby sitters, she stated. My friend thought this would provide a good opportunity to observe the interaction between mother and child so he said he had no objection. Throughout the session the mother fondled her son. In telling me about it, my friend said, "You know, the best way to describe what went on is to say that it came as close to foreplay as anything I've ever seen."

If your mother was overly protective of you, it's possible that you have become unable to make choices, lack self-reliance and have difficulty dealing with problems. Since your mother regarded you as unable to take care of yourself, it's possible that you accept that perception as your own.

Overindulgence. If you perceive yourself to be demanding, selfish, and "spoiled," chances are that one or both of your parents made a big thing of catering to your every desire no matter how whimsical. When I see children who refuse to accept authority figures and rebel against established rules, I have a pretty good notion that the child comes from a home which is overindulgent. Such children are skillful at playing one parent against the other if that's necessary to get their way; so as adults they are equally adept at manipulating others and using them to gain their ends. Oddly enough, overindulged and socioeconomically deprived children have, in my experience, something in common. Neither is able to defer immediate gratification in favor of long-term goals. In other words, they want what they want when they want it.

When the overindulged child reaches the age when he leaves home and meets the world head-on, he retains the perception that he is "the greatest," the most important person in the world. He soon finds out that he really isn't until he proves he is. That's a difficult reality to deal with, and maladjustment of personality is almost assured. The overindulged child also has a faulty sense of values because he's never had to work to get anything.

Other patterns. Other conditions in the home during childhood which lead to poor personality development include persistent *parental arguments* which may or may not be violent; *separation* or *divorce* (which are often better than constant bickering); parents who set *poor examples*; and other home influences which are neurotic in nature. I have mentioned the *double-bind* situation where parents make contradictory demands on the child, forcing him, for example, to feel that he's bad if he doesn't display affection for them, then rejecting him when he does.

Each of us has psychological needs which we strive to meet. At times we must resort to defense mechanisms to meet those needs. Defense mechanisms are designed to help us avoid devaluing ourselves. While there's no need to list all the defense mechanisms—some seventeen of them—the pertinent point is that we have a need to defend ourselves against psychological devaluation. As Coleman says, "We must think well of ourselves and feel adequate to deal with our problems if we are to maintain our psychological integration. Again and again in tracing the development of mental illness, we find severe self-devaluation playing a crucial role."[4]

Experiences which tend to be self-devaluing include failure, loss, feelings of inferior status, loneliness, the feeling that one's life "has no meaning," feelings of guilt, and negative experiences which concern personal factors such as appearance, intelligence, and talents. These self-devaluing influences cause conflicts, and the way one deals with those conflicts determines whether he becomes a person, a self-actualized individual, or not. Conflicts also have a negative effect on our listening. Because identifying them is of vital importance for knowing who and what you are and thus for freeing you to listen totally, I'll list and briefly discuss some of them. Each gives rise to feelings of conflict between what we should do and what we shouldn't do in our interpersonal relationships, and they inhibit communication.

Dependence vs. independence. One of the central conflicts we face during childhood and youth is between dependence and independence. On the one hand is our desire to be free from parental restraints; on the other is the loss of security and the burden of responsibility. Some of us resolve this conflict in favor of dependence. We sometimes hear it said of somebody that "he married his mother" or "she married her father." Some people hide behind psychosis in mental institutions or, when the going gets tough, establish a relationship with a therapist. Increasing num-

bers try to work out the problem by making the rounds of
therapy groups or seek a guru.

Sex. One of the more familiar conflicts concerns the
sexual needs. Masturbation is a normal means of relieving
sexual tension, and it's normal for children to engage in the
practice. As far as the organism is concerned, it's a self-
actualizing device. To the self, however, it often becomes
something different. Many, perhaps most, parents are horrified to discover that their child has a sex drive. In words,
actions, or a combination of both, they show their disapproval of masturbatory activity. The child now experiences
a perception that this activity, which gives him organ-
ismic pleasure, is unworthy and that, therefore, he is unworthy. Masturbation now causes anxiety. There is also
the so-called "oedipal complex," the well-known Freudian
hypothesis that the male child becomes attached to his
mother and the girl to her father.

Sexual conflicts have been further complicated by
societal standards, but these along with parental taboos
are beginning to loosen. The availability of effective contra-
ceptives has made a great difference in the sexual freedom
of youth, but there still remains the question of should.
What is now possible to do without much fear of pregnancy
is still distinguished from what *should* be done. Self-
devaluation can occur when the individual attempts to
fight sexual drives because his parents said sex is evil—
and loses.

Reality. The tendency to avoid "seeing ourselves as
others see us" gives rise to another conflict. The ideal is
preferable to the real if the real is unpleasant. People frequently say "I don't want to hear about it" in response to
bad news. When we don't want to face reality, we go to ex-
tremes to avoid doing so.

In chapter 5 I mentioned the parents with a founder-
ing marriage who used their children to hold it together.
By involving themselves in a continual procession of activities with their children, they managed to avoid facing

the reality that their marriage was in trouble. I have also worked with high school students who wanted to be doctors and lawyers but could read no better than the average sixth-grader. And I have dealt with parents whose goals for their children, given their capabilities, were unrealistic.

We want to be self-actualized—to get input from the environment that says we are what we feel we are. If the reality of a situation doesn't help us with that, we become defensive. We may, for example, project our imperfections onto others.

Fear. In Franklin Delano Roosevelt's first inaugural address he said, "The only thing we have to fear is fear itself." What Roosevelt's precise meaning was, only he knew. But to me he was telling a nation in the throes of economic collapse that we were doomed if we became immobilized by the fear of what might happen.

The conflict between fear, which is a normal feeling, and taking action to solve our problems is a common one. In its milder and more common forms, the conflict is involved in stage fright, a variety of phobias, bigotry, anxiety in taking examinations, and so on. In its more severe forms, it is present in the fear experienced on the battleground, the fear of death, and even the fear of living, as pointed out by Shakespeare:

> Whether 'tis nobler in the mind to suffer
> The slings and arrows of outrageous fortune,
> Or to take arms against a sea of troubles,
> And by opposing end them?—To die,—To sleep,—
> No more; and by a sleep to say we end
> The heartache and the thousand natural shocks
> That flesh is heir to,—'tis a consummation
> Devoutly to be wished.[5]

The soldier facing mortal battle can do so only if he is willing to accept the fact that he is afraid. Unless we are able to accept our fear of situations in our daily lives, we cannot deal with the fear of others; and that also interferes with our ability to listen.

Love vs. Hate. Perls deals with another conflict, that between attraction and repulsion. He uses the psychoanalytic terminology "identification/alienation." In existential philosophy, love is not an entity all by itself but exists only when it has an opposite number—hate. This polarity —love vs. hate, good vs. bad, and so on—is always present. When we say we love someone, we don't mean that we love the total person; we love something, one or more characteristics, about that person. Conflict arises when we discover that there is something about that person that we also hate. This is because we don't say, "I love this part of you but hate that part of you." We say, "I love *you*"; "I hate *you*."[6]

Ethics. A conflict with which draft-age young people had to cope during the Vietnam war was ethical versus societal pressures; should they refuse to fight because they believed the war immoral, or should they give in and fight because to do so would mean social approval?

Some individuals resort to "situation ethics." To smoke marijuana and drive is dangerous to others and therefore unethical; to smoke it socially is not dangerous to others, therefore ethical. The situation is the determiner.

There is ample evidence among our nation's elected officials of the struggle to maintain integrity in the face of opportunity for great personal and financial gain. And every year at income tax time each of us must decide whether to pay the full amount due or look for ways to beat the system.

Values. Closely tied to the question of ethics and other conflicts is the matter of values. Values, as noted earlier, are of special concern because traditional ones are in a state of flux and transition. Young people tell their parents that the old values are not acceptable because they don't work or because they're no longer necessary in the new age of science and technology. Parents mistakenly take that to mean they should "throw out the baby with the bath water." The effect if they do is that the young are left without any value structure to hold onto.

Unclear values prevent total listening because they get in the way of self-acceptance. In order to accept, we must know what we're accepting about ourselves and about others.

This chapter has discussed patterns of child-rearing and conflicts that result. As we proceed, you should be aware of the patterns of parent-child relationships and the conflicts which you experienced as a result. Try to relate them to your own childhood and youth and especially to what you are here and now. Your idea of how your parents felt toward you and the manner in which you deal with your conflicts cause blocks in your ability to relate to others. They are the basis for your feelings concerning what you *should* do and what, in fact, you *do*; how you feel and how you think you should feel. The "should vs. do" difficulty will be detailed in chapter 9 when we look at your emotional style and see how your range of feelings becomes limited.

In chapter 7 we'll look at the ways in which schools contribute to poor listening habits and to the formation of self-perception.

7

"Teacher! Teacher! Billy's Dog Gots Puppies!"

Even though I was an only child, I belonged to a big family. My mother and father came from large families, and we were all very close. On such special days as Thanksgiving, Christmas, and Easter, everyone would bring a special dish, and we kids could be counted on to overindulge. Turkey and stuffing, pies, apple cider, candy—we ate everything. The expected result always followed. At least one of us would have a stomach-ache. Then Uncle Mac would get out the castor oil and force two tablespoons of the stuff down the sufferer's throat. I'm sure that Uncle Mac could have used any one of a dozen other medicines which would have been acceptably palatable. But castor oil was the "medication of choice" precisely *because* it tasted terrible. Even today with the capability of making any medicine taste delicious, drug manufacturers do not. The idea that a medicine is good for you if it tastes bad is so deeply embedded in our culture that many medicines are still made to taste unpleasant.

What that has to do with the subject under discussion is this: the same idea apparently governs the way chil-

95

dren are educated in many schoolrooms I've visited. In order for school to be beneficial it has to be unpleasant.

I'll admit that for some teachers and some kids, silence and chairs and desks all in a row seem to work. But I think the reason they work is that the teacher is happy, not that the kids are. If the teacher has a supervisor who insists on strict regimentation and quiet and that fits the teacher's way of doing things, then he or she will be happy. The teacher's happiness thus sets the tenor of the classroom.

But what if the supervisor's insistence that children remain in their seats and not talk isn't consistent with the teacher's personality? In that case you've got an unhappy teacher and, I'll wager, a roomful of unhappy students. In any situation, it's not what's there that causes you discomfort, but what you bring into it. Teachers have told me that on days when they are "down" or out of sorts, the noise level is measurably lower in their rooms.

To a psychologist, learning means that change has occurred in the learner's behavior. Learning requires intake from a book, tape recorder, teacher, another person; any of these can produce learning and therefore a change in behavior. But real psychological growth requires more than just intake; it requires interaction and (here we go with that word again) acceptance of self and others. As I said, I'll concede that for some kids and teachers the regimented classroom is a viable solution to learning. But I don't see how it can be a psychological growth medium for either teacher or children.

I've mentioned the school in San Diego that I visited. With the kind of freedom to *be* that the children had there, the psychological growth was so obvious you could almost see it. One enthusiastic mother told me, "You know, the thing that my children have gotten from this experience is the ability to be independent. They're self-confident. Under the old system [i.e., the regimented kind], my older children didn't get that."

But experts are already working on the educational system from both directions, so we'll proceed to the matter of how schools help produce schizophrenic listeners. Since we know the listening problem we're concerned with lies in the failure to get behind the words—the content—of messages, let's examine the way language is acquired. It's fascinating to watch a child learn to use language. Just how it happens has been puzzling thinkers since Aristotle. One debate persists.

Behavioral psychologists, most notably B. F. Skinner of Harvard, believe that the "tabula rasa" theory is correct—that at birth the child's mind is a clean slate, that he learns language by interacting with his environment. Children hear sounds, imitate them, and are given reinforcement by pleased adults.[1] It's no accident that the words "mama" and "dada" enter the child's vocabulary so early.

The other side of the debate is carried by psycholinguists such as Noam Chomsky at the Massachusetts Institute of Technology. According to psycholinguistic theory, children are already programmed to develop the principles of language when they are born. Even before a baby says its first words, it has the inborn mental structures with which to build an abstract rule system or grammar of whatever its native language happens to be.[2]

Dan Slobin, at the University of California, Berkeley, has identified some universals in children's language development:

1. They tend to hear and imitate word endings first. An example is "ghetti" for "spaghetti."
2. They are conscious of the order in which the parts of an utterance occur. A child who speaks English learns that "happen" is correct but "penhap" is not.
3. At the start they will avoid rearranging words—for example, to form a question. They will say "Tommy can play?" rather than "Can Tommy play?"
4. They will avoid any exceptions to rules. The irregular verb "run" in the past tense is "runned."[3]

To Slobin, the question of what part of speech a child's word becomes in the adult language is unimportant. What is of interest is the role that word plays in the child's language system. "It seems clear to us now," says Slobin, "that children form a variety of word categories of their own—based on the functions of words in their own language system—and so words must be looked at in the light of the child's total system. . . ."[4] I believe that one message for us in Professor Slobin's statement is this: when adults—school figures included—interact with children, a reality may exist behind what the child says that his words don't imply on an adult yardstick. To understand a child, you must walk in his shoes for awhile.

Teachers often do terribly frustating things to children without meaning to. I've heard this scene enacted on several occasions: Recess is over, and the second-graders are lining up to return to the classroom. One of them, let's call her Lucinda, races ahead of the others to meet Mrs. Nice, the teacher, who is coming down the corridor to meet her class.

"Mrs. Nice! Mrs. Nice! Guess what!" gasps Lucinda.

"I can't guess," Mrs. Nice says to Lucinda. "You'll have to tell me."

"Billy's dog gots a whole lot of puppies, and his mother said . . ."

"Billy's dog *has* a whole lot of puppies, Lucinda. Now what were you going to tell me?"

Why couldn't Mrs. Nice have lived up to her name and responded to the feeling that Lucinda wanted so desperately to share with the third most important person in her world? Was the correct verb all that important? I think that if Mrs. Nice meant her response to be a learning experience, she succeeded. What Lucinda learned was that teacher wasn't really interested in sharing her excitement. What's more, Mrs. Nice wasn't a good listener.

If schools do such a poor job of communicating with children and teachers do such a poor job of describing their feelings, it's no wonder that children don't learn how to listen. The first change that needs to occur is for teachers and other school people—all of us, in fact—to begin saying what we mean and what we feel. The second change concerns the other side of the coin. We need to begin helping children describe *their* feelings. The best way to do that is to start attending to their feelings, to begin "listening to heartbeats."

Primary-grade children assume that they can rely on the fact that what teacher says is what she means and that her actions correctly indicate her feelings—a mistaken assumption, as we have seen. But a teacher should know enough not to make the same assumption about what her pupils say and do. Their actions and feelings are often not congruent. This can lead to frustrations, pent-up emotions, and eventual explosion; and often does.

School is a completely new experience for children, an introduction into a strange world where new rules and restraints are imposed. Suddenly it is no longer tolerated when they simply take something from another child, leave their seats at will, or go to the bathroom when they feel they need to. Now they must "request," "let the teacher know," or "get permission." Words, rather than actions, are now the key to satisfying their wants and conveying their feelings. Teachers (and parents) demand that children communicate with words even though they themselves are demonstrably terrible at doing so. For don't we live by the adage "actions speak louder than words"? But children aren't quite ready for the changes imposed on them in school.

When Billy walks down the aisle of his first-grade classroom and accidentally bumps into Mary, Mary may respond by planting a solid clout on Billy's retreating back. An uncomplimentary remark usually accompanies the blow. This is often followed by something equally uncomplimentary directed toward Mary by the teacher from the front of the room, eliciting a gleeful grin from Billy and a veritable "screaming tizzy" from Mary. What Mary didn't know was that Billy bumped her accidentally. Still being a "doer" rather than a talker, she didn't stop to question his motives. She acted. What the teacher didn't know was that before the bumping incident, Mary had been diligently working on her assignment and was pleased with her neat paper. The bump tore a hole and ruined it.

At that point, had the teacher used her own language skills and her knowledge that children don't have these skills in the first grade, the ensuing horrible scene could have been avoided. She should have used what the behavior modification people call "proximity control." She should have moved immediately to the point of action. To control situations at a feeling level, words directed at the children from the front of the room are usually ineffective. The teacher's immediate physical presence serves to prevent exacerbation of the situation.

Having put a lid on the combat and directed the attention of the class back to its assignment, the teacher can now take Billy and Mary aside and analyze the encounter.

"What did Billy do that caused you to hit him, Mary?" Then, following the reply, "You were very annoyed because your paper was spoiled" (a reflection of Mary's feelings). "There's another paper on my desk, and we still have time for you to do another. I'll help you if you like."

"Billy, what would you like to say about this?" Then, reflecting his feeling of helplessness, "Yes, Billy, sometimes we cause things to happen without really meaning to."

Here's another situation: A class enters the cafeteria. Suddenly, right under the watchful eye of the teacher and cafeteria monitor, one boy shoves another. It's Johnny again! He's been baiting the teacher and his classmates all morning and was scolded for it every time. Why does he persist? Surely, the teacher muses, he doesn't like being reprimanded.

Oh, yes he does, if he's starving for attention and gets it following his every annoyance. His teacher was reacting each time with words directed not toward Johnny's feelings but toward his action. And so his basic need remained unmet. At the first instance of attention-getting behavior, the teacher should have recognized Johnny's need for someone to acknowledge his existence; for someone to provide feedback which would give him the feeling that he is "O.K." Like a comment on his work: "Those arithmetic problems are copied very neatly, Johnny. It's a pleasure to read a paper like that."

Teresa needs help, too. Tears streaming from her eyes, she runs up to the teacher on yard supervision and sobs, "Nobody likes me." She is told, "Of course they do, Terry. Everyone likes you. You're just imagining things. Now dry your eyes and go play."

Having thus been informed that she is hallucinating and having been rejected by yet another, Teresa wanders off, still crying, still feeling unliked and unwanted, alone in her misery. If only the teacher had recognized that Teresa wanted her to know that at that moment she felt totally unloved, the teacher might have said, "Sometimes we feel as though nobody likes us. Would you like to talk about it?"

If Terry says "No," then the teacher could say, "All right, Terry. Would you like to walk with me for awhile?"

Little Timmy, another first-grader, arrives in class with a badly scraped and bleeding knee. He fell in the gravel because he was running to avoid being late. He is crying because he is in pain and because he's frightened. His teacher greets him with, "How many times have I told you not to run!" (a statement rather than a question). Then she follows up with, "I don't know what you expect me to do about it. You'll have to go to the office." That's her one-two punch.

Timmy need not have been made to feel he is an archcriminal. He wanted the teacher to know he feared being late, he is sorry he broke the no-running rule, and his knee hurts. Had she perceived his feelings, she could have said,

"I know your knee really hurts, Timmy. I'll send someone with you to the office to have it bandaged." With Timmy's most immediate needs taken care of, the rule infraction can be dealt with more effectively at a later, less emotional time.

In each case cited, the children were trying in the only way they knew to let someone know they had hurt feelings. Because they didn't have the verbal skills or social sophistication to communicate their feelings in accordance with adult standards, they were driven to inappropriate action. Words are teachers' stock-in-trade. Small wonder then that teachers communicate with children mostly on a verbal level. But when you see how one-sided this arrangement is, you can understand why children often resort to temper displays and other sorts of "acting out" behaviors.

Am I saying that teachers shouldn't use language with children? Of course not. Children are in school to learn to listen, talk, and comprehend, and I'm not suggesting that adults go around shrugging their shoulders at them rather than using words. But I would like to see a change in the tone and direction of those words. Let me give you an example or two to explain why I think a change is needed.

On the first particularly cold, blustery school day of last year, I overheard two third-graders conversing in a school office.

"I bet this is the day Billy is supposed to come back to school," said Reddish Blond Freckle.

"Yeah," replied Skinned Nose.

"Billy who?" intruded the visiting "shrink."

"Billy Jones," chorused Freckle and Nose. "He got in trouble from the teacher and got sent home."

"How do you know he'll be back today?" I pursued.

"Because when Mr. Gray [the principal] took him out of class, teacher said it would be a cold day when he came back to her classroom."

The children could not know that what the teacher

had said was not what she meant and not to be taken literally. This story is a good illustration of one of my pet themes. For children, especially those in the early grades, the adult world is a bewildering place which rotates on an axis of often meaningless words. First at home, then later in school, adults say things to them which are incomprehensible at worst, misleading at best.

Here's a gem directed at a seven-year-old by a frustrated teacher: "I told you to grow up, now grow up!" Instant maturity.

Here's one you could hear in a classroom any day in any part of the country: "Sit down, Bobby. Nobody said you could get a drink." If my experience is any criterion, Bobby will be one thirsty kid before anyone thinks about telling him he should get a drink.

"Don't dilly-dally," Mary's teacher calls after her as the little girl leaves for home. Dilly-dally? What does *that* mean?

"My daddy told me to be have," one second-grade champion pugilist informed me. "So I'm being have."

"Did he tell you not to fight?" I inquired.

"Nope, he just told me be have."

We adults often expect children to be psychiatrists. If not, why would we expect an answer to such a question as "Why did you do that, Karen?" How many grown-ups know why they do a lot of things? Usually "why" questions elicit "because" answers. The point, of course, is that we need to remember that talking with children requires simple words and clear sentences.

For some reason, adults frequently like to play games with children who misbehave, For instance, the teacher who told her pupil to "grow up" knew exactly what the boy had done to irritate her, but she neatly concealed the knowledge from him so that even if he had wanted to stop it, he couldn't. If his sin was running in the corridor, she might better have said, "Running in the corridor is not permitted. You should walk." When Bobby wanted a

drink, the teacher might have been much more effective if
she had said, "Please sit down, Bobby. You know our rule;
if you want a drink, you must ask me first." First, of course,
it's necessary to establish a class rule so that all children
know that they raise their hands to get permission. "Don't
dilly-dally" would be much better and more effectively expressed as "Do not stop on the way home."

Telling a child to "behave" may seem a reasonable
direction to give a primary-grader; it's clear enough to an
adult. But six, seven, and eight-year-olds are not ready for
such abstractions. If a child is a habitual fighter and you
want him to stop fighting, telling him to behave isn't going
to do it. "I do not want you to fight" may not do it either,
but it will come a lot closer. Behaving and being good are
really quite profound ideas if you stop to think about
them. I'm reasonably sure that somewhere a philosopher
is still pondering the meanings of goodness, truth, and
beauty.

It would help if adults would remember that children
approach language in a very pragmatic manner. Until they
get to school, most of their language use is concerned with
obtaining their wants. Once they begin socializing with
other children, they develop sufficient communication skill
to meet their needs in that direction. But once they're on
the educational treadmill, it becomes a whole new ball
game. Now their language use is an end in itself. That's not
an easy thing for children to understand. As we've noted,
experts now think that children have their own rules for
language. But schools attempt to teach rules which run
counter to the child's own.

Another theory proposed by linguistics specialists is
that the child's growth in language is dependent on his
cognitive growth. There appears to be a connection between the way the child gradually integrates more and
more of the details in his environment and the way he constructs a grammar of his language. If that's true, educators
will have to restructure the language curriculum of the

early years. Jean Piaget has shown that the underlying cognitive development proceeds in substages that are quite closely tied to chronological age.[5]

Schools are concerned with teaching children to think —although some critics feel that they don't do enough in that area—and the assumption is that vocabulary acquisition must begin in the primary grades. But words are not needed in order to think. People who are deaf, such as the famous Helen Keller, are perfectly capable of thought without words. We also know that we can express our feelings without words and communicate quite well by gesturing. Our thought processes are closely linked to our emotions and to visual imagery.

Schools would do well, I believe, to defer concerns about vocabulary until the fourth or fifth grade, when the so-called "content subjects" require larger stores of words. Attempts to increase vocabulary have been notably unsuccessful anyway. Those word lists (having no relationship to the child's world) which must be memorized generally aren't—or if they are, they're quickly forgotten. In any case they don't facilitate the child's thinking ability. The time would be more profitably spent on training in listening.

How well do schools train us as listeners? Researchers have found that the average person apprehends only about thirty percent of what he hears and even less of the feeling overtones. Moreover, of that thirty percent he hears, only about half is remembered. There's an interesting paradox connected with that. One of the reasons for poor listening is that we can listen some five times faster than we can speak. In the same time that you say one hundred words, I have the capacity to listen to five hundred. That means I can use the four-fifths of my brain's listening potential to daydream, think of what I'm going to do this evening, reminisce about last night's poker game—or worse, plan my response to your hundred words.

It seems very clear that schools need to devote more time and effort to listening skills. No matter how well-

prepared a presentation might be, the whole thing is useless if those being addressed don't know how to listen.

Unquestionably schools do much to foster poor listening by providing poor models. Egan suggests that the result is that children learn a number of traits which are antagonistic to openness and feeling. They learn:

> How to remain superficial,
> How to build facades,
> How to play interpersonal games,
> How to hide out from themselves and others,
> How to downplay risk in human relating,
> How to manipulate others and endure manipulation,
> How to promote self-interest, and
> How to hurt and punish others if necessary.[6]

In this chapter I've discussed ways in which schools
often continue the poor listening training that children receive at home. Accent is placed on the cognitive factors of
language, not on the affective or feeling factors. Adults frequently play confusing word games with children and provide poor listening models. There is a misplaced concern
with the syntactical rather than with the practical. Rules
are taught—informally, perhaps—which run counter to
those which the child is in the process of developing for
himself. Despite the research which shows that thinking
is a sequential process which can't be rushed, schools often
do try to rush it. At the same time another important skill
is being neglected—listening.

Part III
Feeling, Emotions, and Total Listening

If we fancy some strong emotion, and then
try to abstract from our consciousness of
it all the feelings of its characteristic
bodily symptoms, we find we have nothing
left behind.
William James

8

I Feel,
Therefore
I Am

You may recognize the title of this chapter as a paraphrase of the basic premise of the philosophy of Descartes.
The original version was an assertion that man is not only
a mechanical creature; his difference from other animals
lies in the fact that he is a thinking being. But man is
much more accurately a creature of his feelings than his
thoughts. We are what we feel.

There is almost universal confusion regarding the distinctions between thoughts, feelings, and emotions; and
between descriptions of feelings and expressions of feelings.
Since these distinctions are crucial in the listening/com-
munication process, let's begin this chapter with a discussion of the first difference: that between thoughts and
feelings. Next we'll deal with the difference between feelings and emotions; and finally with the difference between
description and expression of feelings.

To prove to you how easily even the most outstanding
authorities in the field fall into the trap of labeling thoughts
as feelings, let me quote from one author's discussion

about the importance of changing one's perceptions about himself: "Perhaps the facts I have given will make it clear why I feel that we are approaching the point where we can write a genuine equation in this subtle area of interpersonal relationships. . . ."[1]

The words are those of a noted psychotherapist. We cannot, of course, know precisely what his feelings were—perhaps elation, excitement—but the sentence should have read, "Perhaps the facts I have given will make it clear why I *think* that we are approaching. . . ." In using this quotation I mean no impertinence. The author had a perfect right to use the words he did, and I would not presume to question his psychology. But under the laws that govern our interpersonal relationships, it is important that we begin now to watch our own conversation carefully for those thoughts which we mistakenly call feelings.

Let's look at another example. In this dialogue see if you can untangle the thought—feeling confusion:

"Say, Jim, we need someone to work with Harry on the membership drive. As I recall, you worked with him previously. How about teaming up again?"

"No, Fred, I'd like to help out, but . . . well, I feel that Harry doesn't much care for me as a committee member."

What did you make of that? Is that another thought disguised as a feeling? Look at Jim's statement again. Without feedback and a check of our perception, we can't definitely know what his feelings were; but what he should have said was something like, "I *think* that Harry doesn't much care for me as a committee member." He may *feel* uncomfortable with Harry, or he may *feel* disliked by him.

Here's another example: You and Sam are having a drink together after work on Friday afternoon. You are a newcomer, fresh out of graduate school. Sam is your supervisor. You admire him because he got into management without having a college degree, something unheard-of in your line of work. You've always assumed that Sam was very happy in his job, and you tell him so. But Sam turns

to you and says, "Jack, I'm going to let you in on a little
secret. I dislike my job so much that it's an effort for me
to come to work in the morning. I've been doing the same
thing for twelve years. Did you know that? And I feel I've
gone as far as I'm ever going with the company."

If you read closely what Sam said, you will see one
statement of feeling—dislike. But there is another statement: "I *feel* I've gone as far as I'm ever going to"—which
is not a statement of feeling at all. What Sam should
have said was "I *think* I've gone as far as I'm ever going
to." Again, we can't know his true feelings because we
can't get feedback from him, but perhaps his feeling is one
of hopelessness, resignation, entrapment, or even despair.

The title and opening paragraph of this chapter state
that we are what we feel. If this is so, we should be able to
analyze a statement directly from the expressed thought
to the feeling to a description of what the speaker is at
that moment.

For example, in applying that kind of analysis to the
statement "I feel that Barry made the whole team a laughing stock last night," we get something like:

A. I think that Barry made the whole team a
     laughing stock last night.
B. I felt embarrassed by what Barry did last
     night.
C. I am angry with Barry, and I am embarrassed
     by what he did.

(When you can precede a word with "I am," it is generally a statement of feeling, not thought.)

Here's another statement: "We had my new boss and
his wife over for dinner last night. Madge prepared that
dish you like so well. Mr. Smith had two helpings without
much urging, and Mrs. Smith asked for the recipe. After
dinner we sat and talked, and they didn't leave until some-
time after 2 A.M. I felt that Mr. Smith and I hit it off
pretty well."

That could translate to something such as:

A. I think that Madge really helped my carrer last night.

B. I felt pleased with what Madge did to help my career.

C. I am appreciative of what Madge did.

But there was a second, perhaps more pertinent statement (and once again we must make assumptions about the feelings because we don't have the benefit of feedback):

A. I think that Mr. Smith and I hit it off pretty well.

B. I feel more confident in my future with the firm.

C. I am secure in my job.

For a deeper understanding of the distinctions between thinking and feeling, let's consider another distinction: that between feelings and emotions.

I referred earlier to the personality theory called "phenomenology." To the phenomenologist, feelings are based on one's individual perceptions. In other words, my feelings are made up of the way in which I perceive myself, the way I perceive the situations in which I become involved, and the way I perceive the interrelationships between the two.

For most of us in our daily lives, no difference exists between emotions and feelings, and we use the two words interchangeably. But there is a difference. It may seem small, but we will soon see that the ability to distinguish between feeling states and emotional states is very important if we are going to listen and communicate clearly, accurately, and effectively.

We already have a definition of feeling. Here is a brief definition of emotion: Emotion is the physiological aspect of feeling. It is the bodily change—mainly in the endocrine and autonomic nervous systems—which results from the individual's perceptions of himself, of his situations, and of the interrelationships thereof. That attempts to put simply a very complex concept—and, like most such attempts, it requires further explanation.

One can explain the feeling-emotion relationship in two ways. If emotions are bodily reactions and feelings represent one's perceptions, we can assume that a cause-effect relationship exists between the two. Either feelings produce bodily changes or bodily changes produce feelings. For example, one perceives a situation which he feels is dangerous, and the effect of this feeling is bodily arousal to avoid the danger.

While driving to my office one rainy day, I encountered an extremely slippery surface at the top of a freeway on-ramp, just where it merged with the fast-moving traffic. It was like ice. I saw a large truck in the acceleration lane and tried to stop. My brakes were useless. I tried to steer toward the right side of the lane, but the car wouldn't respond. My initial feelings were fear and panic. Just when I was sure I was done for, the truck driver saw my fish-tailing car and quickly moved into the center lane. This gave me sufficient time to regain control of the wheel.

Later as I reviewed my reactions, I was aware that several physiological changes had occurred almost instantaneously. Following the fear and panic feelings, my heart-beat rate increased, my adrenal glands signaled for an increased supply of blood sugar, my muscles were tense, my mouth cotton dry, and my palms and forehead clammy with perspiration. In short, my entire physical system had reacted to cope with my feeling of fear and danger.

William James proposed the reverse situation: that feelings are reactions to physiological states.[2] In his theory, for example, an individual experiencing a stimulus which he perceives as tear-jerking cries. Crying causes him to feel sad. One who perceives his appearance before an audience as a fearful stimulus experiences knee trembling and shortness of breath and becomes afraid. Or a man becomes angry because he strikes another; and so on. This theory, known as the James-Lange theory (although Lange, a Dane, published it independently a year later than James), has been tested and rejected by other psychologists. One experiment, for example, showed that when hormones related to the emotion of fear were injected into volunteers, the subjects reported that although they felt *as if* they were afraid, the feeling was not the same as actually being afraid. As new approaches are made to the study of feelings and emotions, it becomes more and more evident that, although James was correct in saying that bodily states play a role in emotions, such states do not precede them. It's not vitally important that we know which comes first, emotions or feelings; but it is important that we remain aware that feelings are not emotions.

Almost all of what we describe as our feelings concern our awareness of our physical state at the moment. One's bodily state can never be left out of his perceptions. If, for example, I say to you, "I feel just a little anxious about my appointment with the dentist," I am describing the totality of my perceptions at that moment, including my bodily state. I may be a bit short of breath, unable to remain quietly seated, or may even make more frequent trips to the bathroom than usual.

Many of our common expressions demonstrate the close relationship between our feelings and our bodies or bodily states. "He's a pain in the neck." "I really got weak in the knees." "He's two-faced." "She ought to stand on her own two feet." The feelings which might lie behind those respective statements are "I'm annoyed by him," "I was very frightened," "I am distrustful of him," "I'm burdened by her dependence."

The words hate, rage, loathing, terror, ecstasy, joy, elation, sadness, and delight convey clear bodily states to the listener; thus they and words like them are also useful (if we attend to them within ourselves) in clarifying our own feeling states during a conversational interchange. They clearly indicate where we're coming from as well as where the other person is coming from. (As we have already seen, most of us don't have a readily accessible verbal or experiential store of feelings.) What we try to communicate by our feelings, then, is the total picture of our perceptions at the moment, including our bodily state or emotion. Feelings differ from emotions because they are symbols of the *total* perceptual field. Feelings always include emotions as an essential factor of that total perception, but, generally, the circumference of one's feelings extends far beyond the circumference of one's emotions. Emotions, in other words, are a part of feelings.

Recalling that our goal is to improve listening and communication, we must pay attention to the manner in which we deal with our feelings and emotions in interpersonal exchanges. Let's assume for a moment that you are a teacher and I'm one of your students. You are giving an examination. Just as you walk past my desk, I pick up the answer sheet, crumple it, and toss it toward the wastebasket.

"Why did you do that?" you demand.

"Because I felt like doing it!" I reply.

"Well, just because I feel like it, I'm sending you to the office, and you can explain to Mr. Ogre, the vice-principal, why you did it!"

Now if I were impertinent and foolhardy enough at that moment to ask you what you meant when you said that you felt like sending me to the office, you would probably reply that you had made it perfectly clear. Actually, though, it is not your feeling that is clear, but the accompanying emotional state. More than likely you were experiencing and displaying (expressing) the bodily state that goes with the feeling of anger. By failing to convey that feeling clearly to me, you actually fled the scene and closed the door to what might have been a constructive interchange. Let's see how you might have handled it instead:

"Why did you do that?" you inquire (not demand).

"Because I felt like doing it!" I snap defensively (not reply).

"I'm angry that you threw your paper away, and I'm disappointed by your attitude." (You acknowledge your feelings.) "It seems as though you're upset." (You indicate awareness of my feelings.) "I'd like to talk with you after class about this. Perhaps a make-up exam is possible," you say with reasonable calmness. (You seek a common ground.)

That alternate handling of the situation offers the possibility for a sharing of feelings. Don't suppose, however, that full sharing will result merely because the door was left open. What I felt in that situation was an internalized experience. Just how much of our feelings we wish, or are willing, to share will depend on what Buber called the "between" which you as teacher and I as student will establish.[3] A complete sharing of feelings seems unlikely, since our feelings are not even fully available to ourselves. What I choose to reveal of my personal world may come close to the feelings I possess; but even with full intent to convey to another the totality of my perceptions, it is unlikely that I can do so. No language begins to have an adequate vocabulary to permit it.

Another aspect of the difficulty (and one with which we come to grips in this book) is one that was previously pointed out. We devote much energy and effort in trying to preserve the privacy of our internal world. The feelings we actually have and the feelings we reveal to others are not the same. But the scope of my feelings which I'm willing to share with you and the depth to which I'm willing to reveal them can be expanded, as I've also pointed out. We can meet in that area of the between, and together we can decide to expend our energy and effort in enlarging it. But this demands that I extend every effort to become aware of your reality. I can rely only on myself to do that. All I can hope for is that you will reciprocate.

Another reason why the sharing of feelings is important is that they are not within one's control. We perceive,
and immediately we feel. Let's suppose, for instance, that
you perceive that someone you trust has caused you damage by telling a deliberate lie about you. Immediately you
react with a feeling of anger and, most likely, a feeling of
hurt. You turn to a friend standing next to you, and he
says, "That was a rotten thing for Joan to do." You reply,
"I guess the best thing to do is tell her just how I feel
about it. After that I'm just not going to think about it."

You have correctly recognized that you can control
your thoughts about the situation, and you can plan some
sort of action; but your concealment of how Joan's words
made you feel can't be controlled. If you are sad and some
well-intentioned person says "Don't be sad," in no way can
you thereupon say to yourself, "O.K., I'm no longer sad."
All you can do is flee from wherever you are and go to a
place where there is laughter. You can attempt to avoid
thinking about the fact that you're sad, but you will still
be sad.

Because words are not the only medium for communication, recognition of the fact that we can't conceal
our feelings becomes even more important. The bodily
states produced by our feelings give us away because,
whether we want to or not, they cause us to communicate
nonverbally. We can understand much about how others
feel by observing their behavior (including their verbal behavior), and we can make inferences about what they're
feeling. Our inferences may be completely inaccurate, of
course, but sometimes nonverbal behavior provides a more
accurate reflection of feelings than do words. When we are
uncertain as to the other's true feelings, his body language
generally provides the better way to "swing into him,"
place ourselves in his shoes, *empathize* with him.

There are two levels of nonverbal language. Bodily
states, already mentioned, may give away our inner feelings through such physiological signs as sweaty palms,

blushing, and trembling. Even when we reply to "You don't mind, do you?" with a "No," our flushed face may indicate that our true response should be "Yes, dammit, I do mind." We have been conditioned, in ways that we have seen, to permit our thought—that one shouldn't really mind—to govern our reply. Our thought and our feeling are incongruous.

But that's not the only incongruity we must face. Still another will probably creep in and further confuse things. When we attempt to conceal our feelings behind a contradictory verbal message, not only bodily changes give us away. Some sort of action will also betray that we are not revealing our actual feelings.

Let's suppose, for example, that you are seated in a room alone with another person. For the past five minutes that person has been discoursing upon a subject which you found of absolutely no interest beyond the first thirty seconds. You've been looking around for some way to escape.

"...and so that's the reason perfumes are so expensive. Don't you think that's interesting?"

"Oh, yes," you reply, "very." As you say those words you're doing your unsuccessful best to stifle a yawn. Your actions are incongruous with your words. You were inattentive, and you finally yawned.

Another example: You have acquired a certain book after much searching, and you left it on your desk so you could read it during your lunch hour. In your absence a coworker noticed the book and borrowed it, leaving a note that she will return it later in the afternoon. You are strongly irritated. After lunch you chance to meet the borrower in the corridor.

"Oh, Carol, I left a note on your desk that I had borrowed your book. I hope you didn't mind."

How would you reply? You're still steamed, but you might say (as your face reddens), "No, that's all right." Your words are spoken through clenched teeth. The borrower is confused by your contradictory messages. Does

Carol really not mind? she wonders. Are the red face and clenched teeth caused by some aggravation that has nothing to do with me? Or do they indicate that Carol resents the fact that I took the liberty I did?

All confusion could have been avoided if Carol had relied on a description of her feelings or if her co-worker had responded to the nonverbal parts of the message she perceived. In the first instance, here's what could have resulted.

"Oh, Carol, I left a note on your desk that I had borrowed your book. I hope you didn't mind."

"Yes, as a matter of fact, I was very irritated. It took me a long time and a lot of effort to get that book, and I was planning to read it during lunch today."

As Carol utters those words, she accomplishes several things. She makes her feeling, bodily state, and actions congruent. But most important, because she was aware of her feeling she was able to own it—to say "*I* was irritated." She did not say "*You* had a lot of nerve" or "*You* had no right." Such accusatory statements, even if true, have negative effects on interpersonal relationships because they push the accused into a defensive position and shut off communication. But it isn't very often that one can get this kind of straight reply. It could come from someone who has read this book—but let's face it, not everyone will.

Let's replay the same scene, but this time with the second alternative. Let's assume that Carol was unable to describe her feeling. Instead she expressed how she felt nonverbally, and her co-worker responded to that. The exchange could go something like this:

"Oh, Carol, I left a note on your desk, etc. I hope you didn't mind."

Carol, face red, teeth clenched, said, "No, that's all right."

Noting the contradictory physiological action and verbal messages, the book borrower (who fortunately has read this book) responds to what are probably the more

accurate reflections of feelings—the nonverbal expressions
—and checks her perceptions.

"You seem upset about something, Carol. Are you?
I'll bet you were planning on reading that book yourself."

"Well, as a matter of fact I did want to begin reading
it during the lunch hour, and I was irritated when it was
gone."

"Gosh, I'm sorry, Carol. I should have asked first.
Next time I will. It's a bit late, but let me get the book for
you right now."

That's an example of the exact opposite of schizophrenic listening. Carol's fellow worker listened to both the
verbal and nonverbal messages, and by being aware of
what was being expressed she was able to get Carol to describe her feelings. She read Carol's feeling as one of upset.
While she wasn't exactly sure how Carol felt behind the
nonverbal message, she checked her perception by asking
for feedback.

I have suggested that we will seldom get the kind of
straightforward statement of feelings which could do so
much to improve communications between humans. We
have seen how we become conditioned against disclosing
our feelings; how we go out of our way to conceal from
others our own view of the reality of the moment; and how
others conceal their realities from us. You can resolve to be
more open, to say "yes, dammit" when that's what you
mean; but you can't force others into the same resolution.
The best you can do is to help them describe their feelings.
And the best way for you to learn how to help is to know
the difference between expressing your own feelings and
describing them.

We have seen that feelings can be expressed in several
ways: in bodily changes, in actions, and in words. Bodily
changes may be expressed in pulse rate, breathing, perspiring, flushed face, tears, or tremors. Likewise, actions
such as slapping another on the back, embracing, striking,
averting one's glance, shrugging the shoulders, or clenching

the fists are expressions of feelings. Words too can express feelings without actually describing how one feels. Such words might take the form of an *order*, such as "Get out!" Often they are *accusatory*: "You're deliberately attempting to put me down." *Sarcastic* statements are often used to express feelings: "With a friend like you, I don't need any enemies." And we often make *judgmental* remarks: "You're ungrateful" or "You're the most generous person I know."

But none of these statements accurately describes the feeling which prompted them. "Get out!" could mean "I'm so angry with you I can't stand to have you in the room!" "You're deliberately attempting to put me down" might be concealing description of the feeling that "I resented it when you criticized me in front of Melissa." "With a friend like you, I don't need any enemies" might be described by "I was really hurt when you accused me of taking that missing test-answer key."

Another difficulty with making one's feelings known only on the basis of expression is the fact that there is no universal manner of expressing a particular feeling. At one age a boy might express his liking for a girl by pulling her hair or teasing her. At another age he might blush when she is near. Similarly, appreciation may be expressed in words or by presenting a gift. But a gift might be construed as a bribe, even though a feeling of appreciation prompted the giving. Suppose that the giver was habitually embarrassed when presenting a token of appreciation, and his face reddened. That might be taken as an indication of guilt stemming from an ulterior motive.

Thus expressions of feeling can be misleading or inaccurate. When someone speaks to you, you judge what his words actually mean on the basis of his tone of voice, the way he holds his head and body, his hand gestures, and his facial expression. From a stranger, you may make one sort of inference from a particular set of cues; from someone you know, you may infer something completely different.

The situational context also flavors your inferences about the other person's intent. Let me illustrate what can happen.

On a trip to Europe my wife and I, along with some friends, were being guided through Vienna and its environs. As first-timers on the continent, we were continually overwhelmed at the antiquity of the monuments and buildings. That was natural enough for citizens of a nation just celebrating the second century of its existence. But that was a context not shared by our guide, an Italian who was born in Ethiopia; nor was he familiar with my sense of humor. At one point the guide, Erminio, identified a particular structure as having been built in the fifteenth century, so recent in comparison with others we had seen that I chided in jest, "Please don't show us any *new* buildings, Erminio." All of us understood the intended humor because we shared a mutual contextual referent. But Erminio seemed disappointed that we didn't appreciate the tour. I later explained to him—from my frame of reference—what I had meant.

That brings up another problem in the communication of feelings. Our own feelings may lead us to make incorrect inferences about others. Because Erminio was disappointed by my remark, for example, he read my words and my feigned actions (facial expression, voice tone, etc.) as disappointment.

As we have seen, the communication of our own feelings and the understanding of the feelings of others can be extremely difficult and hazardous. But if you are to be a person, it is essential that you assist others in every way possible to understand how you feel; and that you assist others in every way possible to make you understand how they feel. The two efforts are mutually inclusive, and both demand that we give and seek descriptions of feelings.

One way that a feeling can be described is by attaching a label to it: angry, frustrated, put down, irritated, affectionate, happy, pleased, enraged. In the exercise at the end of chapter 3, you tried to find labels and discovered that each of us suffers from a feeling label shortage. On top of that is the inadequacy of feeling words in our language itself.

One step better in describing feelings is to "own" them by preceding them with the personal pronoun "I"— and, where possible, the verb "am." "I am angry," "I am frustrated," "I am put down." Because of the lack of labels, we often augment our feeling words with expressions of the actions that our feelings drive us to: "I'm so angry with my lab instructor I could hit him." Another help in describing feelings is the simile: "I feel like a ship without a rudder." "I feel like a bump on a log." "I feel like I just lost my best friend." "I feel like a million!"

In this chapter comparisons were made between the communicative modes of thought vs. feeling, feeling vs. emotion, and feeling-expression vs. feeling-description. We have seen that because feeling states may surface simultaneously in words, actions, and bodily states (emotions), we may give contradictory messages about how we feel. Our messages, in other words, may be incongruous. The most precise way to express how we feel is to describe our feeling by labeling it. The clearest communication of feeling comes when our words, actions, and bodily states are congruous.

Since we cannot assume that the other person is also striving for congruence, it is up to us to help him—to the extent that he wants us to enter his private feeling world. There are three ways we can help. The first is by demonstrating that we are willing to share our own feelings; the second is to provide and seek feedback; and the third, which is really a part of feedback, is to check our own perceptions. Don't say, "You're upset because I borrowed your book." That's implying that you have psychic powers. A perception check would be, "You seem upset. Are you angry with me because I borrowed your book?" Our perception checks should be "I" statements which are descriptions of how we perceive the other to feel; and a request that the other person confirm or deny our accuracy. "You" statements are to be avoided because they are antagonistic and cause defensiveness in the other person.

In chapter 9 we'll begin to look more deeply into the question of emotions and feelings. We'll deal specifically with your own feeling and emotional style and how it affects your ability to communicate. What we want to know is how limited your feeling-emotion repertoire is and work on expanding it. You'll also gain a better idea of what your own reality consists of.

Let's conclude this chapter with an exercise so that you can check on your learning and can review, if necessary. Answers are at the end of the exercise—but don't look at them until you've decided on your own answers.

1. Decide whether each of the following is a statement of thought or feeling:
   A. I feel that John was misjudged.
   B. I feel that you dislike me intensely.
   C. I'm safe in making that assumption.
   D. I feel sorry for June.
   E. I am frustrated by this assignment.

2. Which of the following are descriptions of feelings?
   A. It's about time you got here. I've been waiting for an hour!
   B. I'm so doggone tired I can hardly keep my eyes open.
   C. If you don't stop, I'm going to make you leave the room.
   D. I'm disgusted with your actions.
   E. I feel that I've been put down.
   F. I have always felt that he was honest.
   G. This is a lot of nonsense.
   H. Sometimes I feel that nobody cares.
   I. I feel that you're trying to exhaust my patience.
   J. Everybody likes Carter.

K. Can you imagine a worse predicament?

L. I feel that this is a waste of my time.

M. You're beginning to get on my nerves.

N. I don't feel that you really care what happens.

O. I'm delighted with the new record album.

P. I feel confident in his ability.

3. Indicate which of the following are *perception checks*:

A. We can all see that you're angry.

B. What are you so furious about?

C. You appear to be depressed. Are you?

D. What I understand you to be telling me is that you'd rather I didn't go along. Is that correct?

E. Well, you're pleased with the results.

F. What did I do to offend you?

G. I get the feeling that you'd just as soon leave. Am I right?

H. Would you like everyone to leave?

I. It seems to me that you'd like everyone to leave. Would you?

J. What in the world are you so nervous about?

K. You look nervous. Are you?

L. I have the impression that you're nervous. Am I correct?

Item K is an inference from the speaker's bodily state, and it is judgmental and argumentative. Remember to avoid that kind of "you" statement. Item L is a much better way of checking the same perception.

Answers:

1. A, thought; B, thought; C, feeling; D, feeling; E, feeling.

2. B, D, E, O, P.

3. C, D, G, I, L.

This above all—to thine ownself be true;
And it must follow, as the night the day,
Thou canst not then be false to any man.   William Shakespeare

9

I Love You,
But Is It All Right
If I Do?

Several years ago I was visiting the home of an acquaintance when his six-foot-four son came home from football practice. The young man went to his father and kissed him on the cheek. His father hugged him. I'll never forget that sight. At first I was embarrassed because such a display of affection was unusual for two grown men and seemed such a personal and private thing to witness. I thought I should not be there. Then I realized that the embarrassment was mine, not theirs. This was their custom when they greeted each other, no matter where they were or who was present. They loved each other, and they never felt a need to stop showing that.

In my experience the two most feared feelings are love and anger. It seems traditional in our culture that beyond a certain age parents and children no longer show or tell that they love one another; and anger is something to be hidden at any age. To be angry is just plain bad.

Along with the current renaissance of man's interest in nature and man's place in it, a new awareness is dawning that man does have feelings and emotions and that there may be nothing wrong with making that fact known to others. Certain awareness workshops are designed to help do that. Their approach is to stress the constructive aspects of letting one's feelings and emotions be known. Here's a typical course description of one such workshop:

"Anger is usually felt as anger *against* and therefore immature, unhealthy and counter-productive. Anger *for* can be energizing and valuable as a way of deciphering what it is that you want. In this program participants explore ways of handling anger through a choosing process, which includes: recognizing feelings and incorporating them into the process, rather than denying them; identifying the real source of your anger, defining objectives; exploring, predicting risks of and choosing options."[1]

As previously pointed out, it is not so much the emotion of anger which is or should be the target of such training—but the feeling which accompanies anger. We know that the emotion or bodily state will surface somehow anyway. The goal is to make the description of how we feel congruent with the bodily state or expressed feeling.

There's something else about that workshop announcement that catches my attention. The course description indicates that the content will include "exploring, predicting risks of and choosing options." There's a calculating implication in those words. If the writer intended that participants should, in the course of an interpersonal encounter or dialogue, explore, predict risks, and choose options, he rules out openness. Only manipulation, not communication, can occur.

Reik put it this way: "The psychoanalyst who must look at all things immediately, scrutinize them, and subject them to logical examination has often lost the psychological moment for seizing the fleeting, elusive material. Here—and only here—you must leap before you look; otherwise you will be looking at a void where a second before a valuable impression flew past."[2]

Other workshops aim at teaching participants to become more assertive, which, when you boil it down, means to be honest about your feelings; not to be manipulative, to say what's on your mind, and to assist others to be more honest and less manipulative toward you. The idea of openness and sharing is there because assertiveness training is based, in part, on existential and humanistic philosophies.

Other courses instruct on problems of sexual expression, particularly in regard to female sexuality. The accent is on the way culture has acted to channel and limit the expression of sexuality, to program each of us sexually. And not only sexually. From birth, through contacts with parents, siblings, relatives, playmates, family friends, parents of playmates, and school, each of us has been programmed in many areas. We have developed a self-concept therefrom. Limits have been set on our feelings and how we can express them. Some we are not permitted to express at all.

Consequently unable to experience or deal with those repressed and limited emotions and feelings as adults, we begin to analyze them. Because anger is taboo, a course is established to teach us the distinction between anger *for* and anger *against*. Through a process of analysis we learn all about anger. What we don't and can't learn from such analysis is the very thing it proposes to teach: anger. Feelings are not cognitive events. Talking about anger isn't being angry.

Sexuality? Workshop participants assume that they will learn how to express themselves sexually and that they will understand themselves as sexual beings. More likely they will achieve the latter than the former. One doesn't become sexually liberated merely by talking about sexual expression.

I have already discussed the conflicts which arise as a result of childhood conditioning: the way we should feel or think we should feel vs. the way we do feel in particular situations. Those conflicts, as we have seen, concern feelings such as anger: either you think you should not feel anger or you think it's O.K. to feel it—to describe it to another or not to describe it. Conflicts also concern sexuality: either it's wrong to have sexual feelings or it's O.K. to have them; to describe them or not. Conflicts result from our programming.

Berne relates the case of a grandmother who taught sexual perversions to her three-year-old grandson. Each morning she would bring him into her bed, where "he would lie in a state of excitement and expectancy" until his mother left for work. He had been instructed to conceal his excitement should anyone come into the bedroom. After his mother had gone, there was "sexual abandon." Having successfully carried his dalliance with his grandmother, one day he attempted to approach his mother sexually as she was drying herself after her bath. The mother was so horrified that despite the child's sexual excitement, he froze in his tracks.[3]

At that point the child became sexually programmed. The traumatic event which produced the programming wasn't his activity with his grandmother but the horrified reaction of his mother. In later sexual situations his feeling that sex is an enjoyable experience conflicted with his feeling that sex should not be enjoyed.

What I refer to as a "program" has also been called "conscience," "value judgment," "the inner censor," and more recently, a "script." But whatever the term used to describe it, the situation is one in which the individual gets his ideas of what he thinks he should feel under the the circumstances from somebody else.

Our programming does not involve only strong feelings and emotions nor does it result only from such traumatic situations as the one described by Berne. Either by design or implication, as previously noted, we come to believe that, across a broad spectrum of feelings and emotions, there are some we are permitted to experience and some we are not. And when we consequently engage in an internal battle, we become so involved in our own reality that we are rendered ineffective as listeners and communicators.

Take, for example, a situation in which Joan meets someone on the street—someone she knows but doesn't especially like because she thinks he never has anything interesting to say. Even as she sees Bob approaching, she has a conflict: She thinks to herself, "I wish I could duck into one of these doorways." But she's been programmed to be polite, so she argues with herself: "I can't do that. I'm sure he's already seen me, and it would be rude."

She wouldn't want anyone to think she's rude, no matter what it may otherwise cost her, so she stops and says, "Hi, Bob, I didn't expect to run into you in this part of town." "If I had, I'd have taken another route," she thinks to herself. "How could I be so lucky." In the meantime Bob has been talking, but Joan wasn't listening.

". . . so I talked to them about it, and I found out I'm in. I'm really looking forward to the challenge!"

"I'm sorry, Bob, what were you saying about challenge?"

Bob has noticed Joan's obvious disinterest and replies, "Oh, nothing important. Well, I've got to run, Joan. So long." And Bob walks away thinking, "Why did I have to run into her of all people? She never listens to anything I say. She wasn't even interested in the fact that the Board made me a vice-president of the firm. I was tempted to avoid her, and I wish now I had."

If these are the kinds of internal struggles going on during your contacts with others, it's more likely that you're listening to yourself than to the other. And it's a good bet that the other person will pick up on that. Bob and Joan missed an excellent opportunity to communicate in that exchange. Had Joan listened, she would have learned an interesting and exciting fact about Bob. He approached her in a state of excitement about his new appointment.

Bob also missed a chance when he didn't sense the conflict in Joan. Each was so involved in personal reality that the other's reality was unavailable. All of us have experienced such situations. They can happen under any circumstances.

I dislike having to speak to an audience. If I could avoid doing so, I would. Unfortunately, my work requires that I talk to groups. In addition, my program tells me that I have a responsibility and that it's wrong for me to try to escape my responsibilities. So I've got an approach-avoidance conflict. The best way to deal with that kind of conflict is to face it squarely. Rather than deny the unpleasant feelings I get when I must address an audience, I've learned to accept the fact that I have them. I can share my feelings with others, and that helps because I find that many, perhaps most, of my audience also experience stage fright. But I can do something else as well.

I talked earlier about the differences between emotions, which are bodily states, and feelings, which are the pleasure or pain associations that accompany those bodily states. I also discussed the need to identify those bodily states or emotions, for we start the process of listening within ourselves by locating those bodily states. Where are they found in our bodies, and what are they?

Schutz points out that only recently has the "importance of body-functioning to emotional states" become recognized. He speaks of the connection between our bodily states and our idioms, some of which I mentioned earlier: "two-faced"; "ear to the ground"; "butterflies in the stomach"; "weak in the knees." Schutz mentions the psychosomatic phenomenon—the discovery that the mind can have an effect on bodily states and the more recent finding that the opposite is also true. "Psychological attitudes affect body-posture and functioning, and his body formation then has a strong influence on subsequent feelings."[4] This is not to be confused with the James-Lange theory which proposed that feelings are produced by physiological states.

Where the James-Lange theory accounted for temporary changes, somatopsychic changes produce long-term "habit patterns."

I'll try to connect Schutz's statement with my stage fright. First, what are the conflicts which give rise to my bodily states? One of them I already mentioned: My program tells me that I have an obligation, but the feelings I associate with public speaking are painful. Still another conflict concerns my self-concept. I was programmed to think that I'm quite intelligent and capable of doing many things well. As noted in the discussion of phenomenology, we strive to maintain and enhance our self-concept. In addressing groups I place myself in a position where my intelligence is "put on the line" and I just might not do well, so I'm tense. My tendency therefore is, on the one hand, to avoid such situations; but on the other hand I know I shouldn't, and I can't.

So here I am with an appointment to talk to a group of teachers. The old stage fright begins to assert itself. First of all I make myself aware of my feelings and the conflicts causing them. I accept those feelings. They're mine, and I can't deny them; doing so won't make them go away. I am tense; I am anxious.

Next I become aware of my psychosomatic state. I am conscious that my breathing is somewhat shallow and my pulse faster than normal. I observe a slight weakness in my knees and a slight tremor in my hands. I note that my hands are perspiring and that my forehead is also clammy. All of those bodily states result from my feelings and my resistance to the possibility that others may not confirm my self-concept.

As I begin to speak, the somatopsychic aspects of the interaction between body and mind become noticeable to me. I become aware that I grip the lectern tightly. I am also conscious that in a very real sense I am using the podium to hide behind. The next thing I'm aware of is that I'm trembling; my voice has a slight tremor as my bodily states heighten my feelings of inadequacy. Trying to maintain my self-concept drains much energy from my performance as a speaker with the result that my feelings tend to become self-fulfilling. I am actually becoming inadequate; I *am* inadequate. I know I am because only an inadequate speaker would be experiencing these bodily states. As I persist in these physical postures, they themselves come to influence my emotional state.

It's a vicious circle. Feelings produce physical posture and function which in turn produce feelings of unease and inadequacy. I have made myself inadequate. The point is, however, that the vicious circle begins and ends with me. As Gunther says, "Tension does not come from outside you; it is something you produce. Excessive tension is a non-verbal message from your body asking you to become more receptive, permissive, to let go and relax."[5]

Now, just imagine that vicious circle at work if, instead of delivering a talk or monologue, you were engaged in a conversation with someone—a dialogue. It's easy to see how that jumble of physiological reactions, feelings, and conflicts would make it impossible for you to get into the other person's reality, to become aware of his emotional side.

Let's begin to become better listeners by acknowledging that our feelings about how we should feel and what we should do are our own perceptions about ourselves. They are not the result of what our parents thought about us or what somebody else thinks about us now; they are what we think they thought. They're what *we* think of *ourselves.* We behave daily in such a manner that others will confirm what we think of ourselves. That works both ways. If we think ill of ourselves in certain respects, we become uneasy when others indicate that they think well of us in those respects.

Writer Leo Rosten once said, that, to many people, communicate means "agree with me." Such people don't really want to have communications with others because it's an invasion of their privacy. To paraphrase, many people don't want to listen because to really listen may be an invasion of their reality. To communicate means to them "listen to me."

Years ago when I first became involved in teaching, I worked in an area where the socioeconomic level of the parents was low. It was a totally new experience for me because I came from a middle-class background and life style. One morning I noticed two boys on the playground were fighting. As a crowd of spectators gathered, I moved toward the fighters intending to break up the battle. A hand gripped my arm and stopped me. I turned and saw the school counselor. "I wouldn't do that," he said. "If you go out and stop those two before they get this out of their systems, they'll just take the fight into the classroom. This is their style—they're actors, not talkers."

Little was known at the time about teaching children how to resolve conflicts, and I assumed that he was right. These kids had been programmed in their homes and community to behave in this way. Fighting was natural to them. Talking out their disagreements was not a natural or normal thing to do. Refusing to cry when they were hit was expected of them. Indications that they were "soft" invited goading and teasing. They had to be physically and psychologically tough in order to survive.

When you're raised in an environment where toughness is the standard, your opportunity to experience the wide variety of emotions at the other pole is severely limited. The effect is inability to deal with tenderness and affection. If you're raised in a home where anger is taboo, you can't handle anger; no model taught you how. So anger is a feeling you don't permit yourself. If you were raised by parents who never demonstrated their affection for one another because their programming didn't permit it, the open showing of affection is probably not in your feeling repertoire. Such early training tends to bind your emotions and your feelings into the typical form of your characteristic reactions—your feeling type. You might be one of the following types:

MR. REAL. Mr. Real is the self-actualized person discussed earlier. If your programming was accomplished by parents who were really open people and completely accepting of others, a good chance exists that you'll be the same kind of person. The more feelings you are open to, the greater your openness to the feelings of others, and the greater your ability to listen and really hear. The more feelings you're open to, the closer you come to being Mr. Real. But most of us place limits on our feelings and so manifest differing feeling types.

MR. TAKECHARGE. Another feeling type is that of Mr. Takecharge, the individual whose interpersonal relationships center around getting other people to do the job. He's an organizer, an executive. He likes to preside at meetings, and he motivates others by promising to give or withhold rewards. But he's not so good at taking charge as he would like to have you think. He can't win the support of others because he isn't open and accepting of them. Mr. Takecharge tends to make bad decisions because he shoots from the hip. He is also threatened when his authority is questioned, and thus he allies himself with those in superior positions to protect his own standing. He wants nothing to do with losers; he has no patience with them and never shows sympathy for their misfortunes.

MR. COMPUTER. A third feeling type is that of the automaton who operates like a data processor. He collects information through a series of questions and is purely concerned with the content of others' messages. He digests data and spews out the synthesized analysis like a robot. Unlike Mr. Takecharge, whose approach is often illogical, Mr. Computer is pure logic. When faced with a challenge to which he's unequal, he withdraws with the implication that the other's communication "does not compute" because the input is defective. He can't abide contradictions. It's important for him to know who is right and who's wrong. Being preoccupied with message content, he has no way to handle either his own emotions and feelings or those of others. He cannot describe how he feels; when angry, he tends to turn crimson above the collar and pound the table.

MR. GOODFELLOW. The fourth feeling type is typified by Mr. Goodfellow. He's the sort who is scared to death of anger and sensitive to it within a square mile. He carries with him a supply of oil for pouring on troubled waters, and he begins a lot of sentences with "After all. . . ." He strives by radiating his own goodness to create an atmosphere in which conflicts just can't arise—because conflicts frighten him. He's also scared to death of being by himself. He'll agree to almost anything, even contradict a previously held position to avoid argument, because he's scared that he won't be liked or will be rejected. He's the individual who needs that assertiveness training mentioned earlier in this chapter. You can count on Mr. Goodfellow to take on your assignment, even if it's a terrible one; then he'll whine about the task to others. He's the office joker and compliment giver, but he has more than his share of "down" days because his attempts to keep the peace are wearing and don't always succeed. He evaluates you on the basis of your altruism and dislikes those who injure others.

As you see, each of these feeling types except the first is so bound up in its own peculiar hangups that access to feelings is cut off. Not everyone will match one of these types perfectly, of course; but in your own self-concept a sufficient number of predominant characteristics will identify you.

Right now I want you to tackle a few more exercises. The idea is for you to learn more about you. Remember, the more work you put into the exercises, the more you'll get out of them; it's up to you.

    1. Determine which of the feeling types you match. I'll assume that you're not Mr. Real just yet—you're working on that. Are you Mr.

Takecharge? Mr. Computer? Mr. Goodfellow? Think carefully, and decide which type characterizes your life.

2. Now that you've made a decision about exercise 1, your next job is to become aware of the direction you need to take in order to become Mr. Real. For example, if you decided that you're Mr. Computer, you're not in touch with your feelings. You're not open enough to express or describe them or to accept them from others—it bothers you when others come too close to you physically or psychologically.

   If you're a Mr. Takecharge, you need to be more tolerant of the mistakes of others and their failure to act as quickly as you'd like. Learn to give help rather than criticism. You may need to work on your habit of making ill-considered decisions too.

   If you're Mr. Goodfellow, learn to say no when you mean no. If others make statements or take actions you find disagreeable, tell them so with a well-phrased "I" statement. You'll be amazed to find that instead of losing friends you'll gain them and win their respect.

3. Next identify several conflicts in your life and begin trying to reconstruct how you deal with them. Then try to recall what incidents in your life programmed your feelings about them. Where did your should-feel vs. do-feel conflicts come from? Begin with your parents and things they said or did which were significant in the following common conflict areas:

   A. Hostility
   B. Sexuality
   C. Honesty/dishonesty
   D. Physical contact (touching)
   E. Ethnic differences

F. Any others you'd like to consider
Can you handle them? Are you open to them?
Can you accept them? If you can, what caused
you to? If you can't, what caused you not to?

4. With the first person you meet, try this: Concentrate on how he or she looks—happy, sad,
preoccupied, hot, cold, tired—and tell that
person what you see. "You seem happy," "You
seem sad," etc. Then compare the effect of
that communication with your usual approach.

5. The following exercise is designed to make
you more aware of what your feelings do to
your body and what your body does to your
feelings. I earlier described my own feelings
about speaking in public. Now I'd like you to
put yourself in that situation. How do you
react? Can you really feel your body? Where
in your body do you feel tension? How can
you tell where those areas are? What conflicts
are you aware of, and how do you deal with
them? Now do the following:

A. Pretend you are actually on a stage. Concentrate on your audience. How does it
look? You'll find it generally friendly and
expectant, interested in what you're about
to say.

B. Now talk to the audience. Tell the people
how you feel about them. Tell them what
you see as you look at them; that you
appreciate their interest.

C. Now check back on your stage fright.
You'll find that it's gone—because you're
dealing with the here and now. Anxiety
exists only when you try to deal with the
unknown future. You're also shifting the
focus from being looked at to looking at;
from yourself to your audience.

6. The next exercise is to make a list of feelings that you don't permit yourself to experience. Become as aware of them as you can, and accept the fact that you suppress them. Keep them in mind.

7. At your first opportunity share these exercises with someone else, and discuss how you feel about each of them.

In this chapter I hope you zeroed in on yourself sufficiently to learn more about how you work emotionally and what kinds of feelings you permit yourself to experience. You should now be able to recognize your feeling style and know something about the areas in which you are a real person as well as the areas where you aren't; and you should have some idea of how to become as self-actualized as you'd like within your limitations.

Chapter 10 will deal with how you can pinpoint your own feelings and those of others by making them concrete. You'll learn about how you communicate in interpersonal relationships, and you'll gain increased awareness of factors which operate to enhance your communication—and of factors which interfere with them.

*When you want to rescue a person from
drowning, you have to jump into the water;
into* his *water. The first conjecture of the
concealed meaning should be from the
emotional side.*   Dr. Theodor Reik

10

It's
the Other Guy's
Marble

Someone once said that the secret of conversing so
that others will think you're very interesting is to pretend
that you're passing a marble back and forth as you talk.
The trick is to put the marble in the other person's hand
and try to keep it there. When I thought about that advice, I realized that the most interesting people I know are
those who do the least talking, the ones who let *me* talk.
They're also the most comfortable to be with because
they allow me to *be*.

One reason why people like dogs is that dogs don't
talk; they just wag their tails. You can read into a tail wag
just about anything you like without fear of contradiction.
As far as the dog is concerned, it's always the other guy's
marble.

Another way to think of that conversational marble
is to imagine it containing all the emotions and feelings
available to the holder. When someone is talking to you,
he owns all the feelings and emotions, and you have no
right to take them. When it's your turn to talk, you have

the marble; you own all the emotions and feelings, and he has no right to take them. There's one more rule: whoever owns the marble at a particular time is not permitted to give the other any of his feelings.

Now let's do a little more imagining and try out that premise. We've established two rules: (1) let the other person do most of the talking, and (2) each person owns his own feelings; each can neither take the other's nor give away his own.

Let's suppose that it's the other person's turn to talk. You can tell from his bodily state, his expressed feeling, that his words aren't accurately describing his feelings. Let's say that his drooping shoulders and facial expression indicate that he's disappointed about something. That's the message you pick up from his nonverbal language. But he's saying at the same time, "It really didn't bother me when Mary did that to me." His expressed feeling and his description of how he feels don't match; they're incongruous. An old song lyric put it something like, "Your lips tell me no, but there's yes in your eyes."

One of two things is going on with that person. Disappointment is a feeling that's not in his repertoire, one that he doesn't permit himself to experience; or it's still in the marble and he hasn't dug it out to show you. If you follow Reik's suggestion, you go with the emotion rather than the words and assume that he's concealing his disappointment at whatever Mary did to him. If clear communication is to occur between you, his expressed feeling and his described feeling need to come together. You could reach into the marble and dig out the feeling for him; you could say, "You're not being clear. Say what you really mean." But that's risky because until now you're operating on an assumption about how he feels. And anyway it's his feeling, remember, and you have no right to it. To tell him he's not being clear is evaluating his ability as a communicator. It makes your reaction the criterion for success of his messages.

You might also come right to the point and voice your assumption. You could say, "Look, I can see you're disappointed." If he's really trying to conceal that feeling from you, he's likely to say, "I just told you I don't mind, now drop it!" I vividly recall making an assumption that one of my co-workers was angry about something that had happened to him, and I made the mistake of telling him so. It was a good prophecy, at least, because he became very angry with me and said, "Look, goddammit, don't ever tell me how I feel!" I never again did. No, that's a violation of our rule: you are not allowed to give the other person your feelings.

That brings us to an important consideration, one that was noted earlier in the anecdote about Sidney Jourard's encounter with the Esalen audience that wanted him to "tell all" about himself. Jourard, you'll recall, informed his hecklers that he was "a private person."[1] Now if I tell you how you feel on the basis of my assumption about your emotion and your feeling expression, I deny you your right to conceal that feeling from me if you wish. It's crucial to understand that openness doesn't mean that you have to tell everything that's on your mind and in your guts. It does mean that if there's something you don't want to reveal, you're open enough to tell the other person that.

At another point Jourard says, "If a patient asks me a question I'd rather not answer, I tell him, 'I'd rather not answer.' I give him true reasons, too. . . . I strive to give the patient an openness of myself at that moment."[2]

Schutz also believes there are times when he should withdraw, when he should inform the group that he doesn't really want to lead and that he'd rather be elsewhere.[3] Invoking your right to harbor feelings or withdraw very frequently may, of course, indicate a problem. I don't know just how frequently you can withhold and refuse to share your feelings before doing so begins to interfere with your listening ability; but it's safe to say that the more sharing there is, the more caring there is. And bear in mind: In order to listen totally, you have to understand yourself; in order to understand yourself, you have to be understood by another; in order to be understood by another, you have to understand the other. All of that understanding requires sharing and openness.

Another thing you must be aware of when communicating with others is your motivation. If you open up only because you want to understand yourself, you may throw caution to the winds and open up to anyone who comes along—and that could be a mistake. An important consideration is that you have the right to choose those to whom you reveal your feelings. Something else that Leo Rosten advised was not to open up to help yourself—because you don't know whether you can trust the other. And Polonius advised Hamlet,

> See thou character. Give thy thoughts no tongue, nor any unproportioned thought his act. Be thou familiar, but by no means vulgar. The friends thou hast, and their adoption tried, grapple them to thy soul with hoops of steel; but do not dull thy palm with entertainment of each new-hatched, unfledged comrade.... Give every man thine ear, but few thy voice. Take each man's censure, but reserve thy judgment.[4]

Nobody can tell you how many people you should shut out and not share with; that's a personal matter. But again, if you shut out very many, it may indicate a problem.

Now let's look at this act of "owning" your feelings. You should have a fairly good idea now where gaps exist in your feeling repertoire and where in your programming those gaps may have originated. You also know to some extent where in your body those feelings manifest themselves. In the analogy of the marble, it is forbidden to give away your feelings. Let's go a step or two further.

In psychiatry the word "reification" is used. When we reify (and most of us do), we turn our feelings, which we know to be internal phenomena, into external entities. For

example, "I can feel the hostility" is a reification and projection of "I am afraid." "I feel a great loneliness" is a
reification of "I am very lonely."

You can see how reification robs us of feelings and
projects them out of us. They are violations of our rule
that we can't give away our feelings. Reification interferes
with communication.

I can't communicate—I can't listen—if I'm busy trying to give away my feelings at the same time. If I am not
interested in what someone is saying, I will continue to
listen and reveal my disinterest through nonverbal language; or I will excuse myself; or I will say, "I'm not interested in what you're telling me." The last is an honest
description of feeling, but the first and second options are
the ones most often taken, so that after you leave, you will
think to yourself—reify—thus: "God, that was boring,"
or, "He's a bore."

Do you see what you're doing? You're giving away
your feeling and projecting it onto me. You've opened up
the marble while I was holding it and dropped in one of
your feelings. What you meant was "I am bored." It's
true, of course, that something about what you heard
caused you to feel bored; but what was it? Was it something in me or in my words? In you? Or in a combination
of these? Let's assume that it was something in me. You
weren't listening to what I said, so it wasn't actually my
words that made you feel bored—and you really had no-
where else to go at the moment.

In Perls' therapy his patients analyzed their own
dreams by playing the part of persons, characters, or ob-
jects that appeared in the dreams and carried on dialogues
with them. At points Perls would interrupt and admonish
that the patient was not really into the dialogue, saying "I
don't believe you. That's just 'literature.' "[5]

Let's look again at that bore. If you're bored because
he's uninteresting, maybe he's uninteresting because he's
talking "literature." In that case you're bored because

you're attending to the content of his words. If only you could say "I don't believe you; you're giving me literature. Where are *you*?"—but you couldn't, of course, and even if you could, he wouldn't know what you meant. What's happening is that your nonverbal expressions of boredom are turning off both of you. Your body reflected your bored feeling, then made you feel more bored. The speaker sensed your boredom and turned off everything but his mouth and his cognitive process. He's giving you "literature" because he's afraid to reveal himself to you—to share his feelings with you. Believe it or not, you're boring him too.

When feeling is added almost anything said will be interesting. I've heard Richard Burton read the telephone book and never heard anything so fascinating in my life. As an actor Burton can be exciting even when his emotions and feelings are not genuine. Even his "literature" is exciting. But you and I are not Richard Burton. In order not to be "literature," our words must be backed by authentic feelings. We can't say "It was a very exciting thing" and make it believable unless we're really excited when we say it.

As a listener your reaction to the speaker can turn his dull words into a real adventure. All you have to do is assist him to turn on his feelings. Get that marble into his hand, and help him dig out his feelings to the extent that he wants to. I've seen many examples of what can happen when one person helps another become aware of feelings.

For about twelve years I was a salesman—"manufacturer's representative" was the euphemistic term we used so customers wouldn't be frightened when we visited. I met some truly dynamic master salesmen on that job. One sales meeting I will never forget.

The company's new national sales manager had flown from New York, and the California sales staff was gathered at the Hotel Fairmont in San Francisco to meet with him. A new product had been added to the "line," but sales had not been as good as expected. In the Fairmont's plush conference room we expectantly awaited the man from the head office. Suddenly, up the aisle toward the podium strode a smallish man in his mid-forties, slightly bald with gray hair at his temples, generally unimpressive—until he opened his mouth.

"I'm here to meet the finest sales team in California," he began, "and as I look at you it's easy to see why you've had such an impressive sales record." He had us captured at that point. He said it convincingly. We believed him and believed in him—and he made us believe in ourselves. Stage fright? Not for him; he was a "here and now" man. He focused on us and our feelings, not on himself and his feelings.

"Yes," he continued, "that's why I'm here. I'm glad to get to know you men. But you know, there's more to my visit than that, and that's what I want to talk with you about today."

He lifted a phonograph record. "This says it a lot better than I could, so I'm going to play it for you." Do you think he had our interest by that time?

He turned and placed the record on the turntable, located the tone arm at the right groove, then flicked the "on" switch. The voice of Frankie Laine filled the room, singing a great hit of the moment, an inspirational song which affirmed the lyricist's belief that the world runs according to a divine plan.

The record played through to its conclusion. Slowly and deliberately the sales manager removed the record. He held it up over his head once more and said, "That song sold a million copies for Frankie Laine. Do you know why? When Mr. Laine sang those words, HE BELIEVED!"

From that point the conference sounded like a revival meeting. A dozen enthusiastic "Do you believes?" from the podium met an equal number of enthusiastic "We believes!" from the audience. Let me tell you that by the time we left that room we were *believers* in that new product. The saying goes that no manufacturer has ever produced as much as is sold at a sales meeting, so I doubt that our subsequent performance matched our ardor—but we certainly did believe! One man had caused a roomful of people to recognize that their failure was due to their own feeling of disbelief in the product, not the customers' disbelief in it. Instead of working with our feelings, that sales manager might have heard each of us give our sales presentation, then picked it apart. But he was a good psychologist, and he knew that our feelings needed to be brought out. The following Monday morning we were such enthusiastic believers that we could have made a sale by reading the stock market report to the customer.

So that's what we have to do as listeners. If you're bored, own the feeling, don't reify it. The speaker probably won't be boring if you help him bring out the feeling behind what he's saying.

There is something else about this business of owning your feelings. Just sticking a label on a feeling, saying to yourself "I feel bored, angry, or whatever," isn't owning the feeling. We learned that you must also locate that feeling in your body. Where is boredom located for you? In your eyelids, forehead, neck, shoulders, stomach? In your left big toe, maybe. But there's something else to do before you own that feeling. Just as you can't say "I feel bored" and really own the feeling, you can't say "I've located the feeling in my left big toe" and do anything with that. Now comes the task of describing what you feel in your toe. Does it ache? Is it numb? Does it twitch or feel compressed?

Locate a feeling right now in your body. Maybe you're tired. Where is that feeling of tiredness located? If it's in your eyes, put everything else out of your mind and concentrate on the way your eyes feel. They burn. The lids are heavy. They feel bloodshot. Get into your eyes. Really feel that burning and the weight of your lids, the scratchy feeling. Concentrate on that for about a minute; really work on whatever part of your body you're conscious of feeling this minute. How does that part feel? Now close your eyes and open them again in a minute or so. Let your mind go into yourself. Go ahead.

Welcome back. I expect that two things have happened: You've had a totally new experience; and your eyes, or whatever part of your body you worked with, no longer feel the same. The point is that you have owned your feeling. Really owning it means that you can do with it anything you want. You're in charge of it—it's not in charge of you. You can turn it off if you want to. You can elect to use it if you wish. Once you eliminate the tiredness in your eyes, you're no longer tired or feel tired. Once you eliminate the boredom in your body, you're no longer bored. Now you can show an interest in the speaker. He senses your interest, and you find that he becomes interesting. It's no longer "literature"; now the feelings come through.

When you understand that your judgments—your evaluations of another person's communications—are really judgments of yourself, you begin to work on that; and merely by accepting it, you begin to change. You suddenly find that people you never thought were good talkers are very interesting. What makes a talk-show guest stimulating to listen to is the host—the interviewer. Why? Not so much because he asks the right questions but because of the way he asks them. He's also a good listener, and he provides a listening model for you the viewer. As previously noted, the most interesting persons we know aren't those who talk but those who listen to us.

Motives, as mentioned, are very important in communication. I've watched television interviews for which the interviewer's staff provided the background information on the guest. Such interviews begin with an uncomfortable feeling, questions in which neither interviewer nor guest has any interest, and it's obvious. The program is dull. But once the prepared questions are put aside and the host moves into areas he's interested in, the guest seems to come alive. The interviewer has helped him turn on his feelings.

One more thing I want to discuss in this chapter is the matter of making your feelings clear. When we deal with feelings, our worst enemy is abstraction. What can we do to avoid abstractions? Since the opposite pole is concreteness, can we learn to make our feelings—our descriptions of feelings—concrete? The answer is yes. Let's examine the wrong and right ways in the following situation.

Bill Driver has been a salesman with the Acme Square Wheel Corporation for six years, having begun his career as a young college graduate. Last week he was promoted to assistant sales manager over a number of competent salesmen with more seniority. Announcement of the action was made to the employees this morning in the form of a memo from the vice-president in charge of sales.

Bob Rider's copy of the memo was on his desk when he arrived at the office. As he read it he became angry because he thought his longer service should have been considered and that he should have been given the job. He also felt frustrated because he thought his failure to receive the promotion signaled an end to his progress with Acme Square Wheel.

That day at lunch he told a co-worker whom he considered a good friend how he felt about being passed over —at least he thought he did. "Everybody knew Bill was going to get to the top in this organization," he proclaimed.

Unfortunately that statement lacks much in communicative value. First of all, it's a generalization. It tells about everybody. Did Bob really have the right to speak for everybody? Secondly, wasn't it himself and how he felt that he wanted his friend to know about? Another major fault of the statement is that it does not describe feelings at all. The friend had to infer how Bob felt from his nonverbal language and his "literature."

If Bob's friend was the new executive's secretary, his

statement might be correctly interpreted as criticism of her boss and might evoke an angry response—hardly what Bob wanted or needed at the moment. If his friend was another eager young salesman fresh out of college, he might construe Bob's words as admiration from Bill Driver. The sales vice-president who selected Driver might think that Bob was merely jealous. Driver's immediate superior, the sales manager, might hear an implication that he'd better be on his own guard lest he lose his job to this up-and-coming new junior executive.

In any case, the waters are still murky and conceal Bob Rider's true feelings about not receiving the advancement. In order to convey his feelings to his friend, he must make his words, bodily states, and feelings congruent. His original statement should have been something like "I'm angry that I wasn't given that position. I'm a good salesman, and I believe I'm better qualified. Besides, I've been with the company longer, and that should count for something. I feel frustrated, too. It looks like I've gone as far as I'm going to with Acme Square Wheel."

That's more like it. There's no generalization in that statement. It clearly speaks what Bob Rider feels. It even lets the listener know precisely why he feels as he does. Inference is neither necessary nor possible.

In previous chapters you worked on becoming aware of your feelings and on expressing them clearly. That's where total listening starts. In chapters 11 through 14 we'll shift emphasis from the art of expressing feelings to the art of listening to the feelings of others and helping them express those feelings clearly. We'll start learning in the next chapter to become aware of others' feelings.

To conclude this chapter, try the following exercise. Tomorrow or as soon as possible after reading this chapter, briefly note each time that you (A) use a generality (e.g., "everybody," "always," "nobody") in talking with others; (B) make a statement ("You never listen to me") without giving a specific instance; (C) fail to use "I feel" or "I am" to describe your feelings.

Continue this exercise each day for a week, and see if you can reduce the number of times you do these things. You'll find that people will become more interesting; and they'll find you more interesting.

Part IV

Let's Go to Work! The Art of Total Listening

If you can't do anything to improve on the silence, don't disturb it.

11

Don't
Just Stand There—
Listen!

I think it's clear by now that listening isn't a passive thing; it's work. I don't know of any harder mental labor than listening to the words uttered by another for the feelings they reveal—or conceal. But if you care, it's a labor of love.

Next time you're listening to someone—really listening—you will discover, if you haven't already, that, hard as it is to attend to that person's words and to reach for the feeling behind them, there's an even harder job. What's really a strain is enduring his silences. How do you reach for the feeling behind silence?

I'll never forget an experience I had in the "fishbowl." That was the name we student would-be counselors gave to the see-through mirrored room inside which we sat to be observed by our professors and peers as we tried out our classroom learning on volunteers.

My first "client" was a delight to work with because he "opened up" right from the start. In my inexperience I believed that he did so because of my skill in applying all the counseling theory and technique I had learned from

classroom lectures and books. I realize now that I had unconsciously assumed our relationship to be a complementary one, with him as receiver of help and me as giver. The
sessions flowed easily because he was willing to accept that
kind of relationship between us. We both believed that he
was there to talk and that I was there to listen; there was
mutual confirmation of roles. In any case he obtained some
helpful insights about himself, and I too learned from the
experience. My second counselee I can't recall. But number
three, well. . . .

Anyone could have seen that this fellow was there to
challenge me. At first I thought he was a "ringer" someone
planted as a joke. He did everything except come right out
and say, "I'd just like to see you help me; I dare you to
try." It was a terrible experience for a fledgling practi-
tioner of the counseling art. With all those people watching, my ship was torpedoed and slowly sinking. Number
three was an expert. He seemed to know that the most de-
vastating thing he could do was not to joust with me verbally; he had a better technique.

"Tell me something about yourself," was my opening
line. That opening had always before evoked *some* response even if only a name and address. He replied,
"There's nothing much to tell."

"Tell me anything at all," I urged. Silence.

Client-centered therapy was in vogue at the time, and
I remembered from my course in counseling theories and
techniques that I shouldn't break the silence.[1] I also remembered the adage "Silence is golden." For what seemed
an eternity (later reported by my observers to be forty
seconds), the two of us sat in that room which was wired
for sound—and there wasn't any. To my chagrin it was I,
not the counselee, who broke the silence. The experience
itself was almost as bad as sitting through the critique of
it by my professor and the other student counselors. But
I learned more about myself and the counselee from that
silence than if he had run on like a fountain.

When you're listening to another and he suddenly lapses into silence, don't break in. It's not wasted time. You can bet that *something* is going on inside him during that silence. You can often gain much more insight while he's saying nothing than when he's talking. His next communication will probably come from a deeper feeling level.

Fill the silence by making sure that you're in touch with your own feelings. Check to be certain that your nonverbal language is saying to the other person, "I'm really in tune with what you're telling me. I want to hear it totally." What do your facial expression, your eye contact, your physical stance tell him about your attentiveness and motivation?

Be aware that the other person has expectations about how you'll act and react toward him. Does he expect you to be friendly toward him? Or does he expect that you'll be hostile? What are you showing him? Are you friendly, remote, hostile, accepting, rejecting? He has expectations regarding your openness. Does he show that he distrusts you? If he feels constricted in the relationship, he may. Does his attitude seem to indicate that he wants to depend on you? Or does it seem that he thinks you want to be one-up in a complementary relationship? Is he indicating that he's responsible for himself, or is he trying to make you responsible for him?

How do *you* see *him*? Is he active toward you or passive? Does he offer to share, or does he withhold and withdraw? Does he seem to accept you, or is his attitude one of rejection?

Let's talk about some of the cues that are available when you listen to someone talk. If you really want to listen, the speaker will provide information about his feelings on several dimensions:

Voice. How does he sound to you? Is his voice overbearing in its loudness? Or is it so soft that you must strain to hear? Be aware that the voice can be used as an instrument of aggression. Does this voice indicate that its owner has great vitality and enjoys life—or is it a flat, un-spirited, and characterless voice? Do you hear tightness in the speaker's throat, or does he seem relaxed? Are his voice tones strident or mellow? Does his speech come rapidly, or is it measured and deliberate?

BODY LANGUAGE. What cues can you get from the speaker's posture, facial expression, and gestures to his physical and psychological state? A shrugged shoulder, a raised eyebrow, eye contact—all provide information about the speaker's feelings.

IDIOSYNCRATIC EXPRESSIONS. Very often a person adopts phrases or expressions which provide cues to his feelings. I have a habit, for example, of ending explanations with "O.K.?"—which I think means "did you get the mes-sage?" or, in some cases, "did you understand the mes-sage?" Either of these tends to make the listener feel that I minimize his intelligence, his listening ability, or both. Other such expressions are the now-famous "I want to make this crystal (perfectly) clear," "to tell you the truth," and "let me say this about that." These may be verbal smoke screens concealing the hidden message. When some-one says "I don't mean to change the subject," you can safely assume that he *does* mean to change the subject. Your question is, "Why?"

MESSAGE VALUE. Much can be learned about where the speaker is coming from by attending to what he talks about. In workshops, most neophytes to sensitivity train-ing limit their conversation to past events, or how they would feel if, rather than to here-and-now kinds of things. They story-tell or, as we have seen, provide "literature." That sort of verbal behavior is defensive, and nothing hap-pens until the speaker begins to talk about how he or she feels—at this time and in this place.

THE GESTALT. As previously noted, man's personality is (or at least should be) an integrated entity, not a frag-mented one. If you attend to the totality of feeling expres-sion and feeling description, body language, phrasing of verbal language, and topical choice, you can obtain valuable cues to feelings.

You now know that in addition to watching for the kinds of cues the speaker provides, attending to his speech —listening—means letting the speaker know that he is at the moment the most important person in the world to you. You can do that by showing that you discriminate among his messages—sort out feeling from content and respond to it. You must show him that you respect him by maintaining eye-contact, for example, and not interrupting his speech. You can reinforce his verbal behavior, his willingness to share his feelings with you, by attending. It has been said that "an averted face is often the sign of an averted heart."[2]

Of all the ways a listener can manifest attention and thereby encourage openness and acceptance of himself by the speaker, the most important is facial expression. What you have to say is of almost negligible importance. The way you say it, the tone of your voice, etc., accounts for about a third of what the other person perceives in you that he likes.

Paul Ekman notes that meanings of gestures are not universal. They vary with cultures just as do languages. On the other hand, many facial expressions are symbolic across cultures. Charles Darwin believed that human facial expressions are biologically based and developed through the process of evolution. Ekman found that people around the world who were shown photographs of different facial expressions correctly identified the emotions represented. "Across nine literate cultures there was agreement on both the identity and the intensity of facial expressions. Even non-literate people of New Guinea could correctly identify photographs of most emotional expressions, and responded accurately when instructed to act out a variety of emotions."[3]

Brian Weiss, reporting on research done by Harvard psychologist Gary Schwartz and his colleagues, stated that "the face is a sensitive tablet on which we record our emotions, and we've learned to become careful readers. The universality of at least some facial expressions suggests an origin far back in our evolutionary past."[4]

It would seem, based on these studies, that Darwin's theory was correct. And that people can judge our feelings toward them by reading our facial expressions also seems true.

So you begin with a facial expression which should help communicate that you really want to hear what the other person has to say and how he feels. Next you adopt a physical and mental set for the listening process. You become aware of all possible cues and of your own body language and feelings. You're ready to listen, and you show it.

When the speaker begins to deliver his communication, there are, as mentioned earlier, many possibilities for listener error. One possibility is error of observation. In a film often shown to beginning psychology students, several persons who are witnesses to a crime are asked to describe what they observed. No two of them report seeing exactly the same things. You literally can't believe your eyes.

During a recent trip, I was recovering some baggage in the Los Angeles International Airport. An elderly Oriental man came through the baggage area making all sorts of strange gestures, as if he were fighting an imaginary enemy. Inquiry revealed that the gentleman wasn't weird at all. He had just arrived from Japan after a long flight and was working out the stiffness in his body by practicing a few judo tactics. There's danger in making inferences on the sole basis of observation.

If I were to approach you with my teeth bared and fists clenched, you might infer that I intended to strike you. But I might actually be angry with someone else and preparing to share my feeling of anger with you. It's fairly commonplace for a person to admonish another for laughing at him only to be told, "No, I wasn't laughing *at* you; I was laughing *with* you."

Now we can't just shut off our tendency to infer from observation of behavior. Like our feelings, our inferences are there—we can't deny them, and they can, in fact, help us in understanding the other person's feelings. But we do need to validate our inferences—to check them out and see if they accurately describe what we think they do.

A wit once remarked that a good counselor need possess only two things: gray hair and piles. The gray hair is to make him look wise and the piles to make him look concerned. I must confess that I once adopted a position during counseling sessions which indicated that I was intensely interested in what the client was saying—when I was actually bored because I was getting "literature." Today I would admit and share my boredom if it could help the counselee. The point here is that the client may have been inferring that I was interested; or I may have incorrectly inferred that he inferred that. Beware of inferences. In order to get into the area of the between, you must check their accuracy. Failure to do so, among other things, places you in danger of taking away the other's feeling.

If the other person yawns while you're talking with him, does that allow you to infer that he's not interested in what you're saying? Maybe it means he didn't sleep well last night. If he leans forward with a pained expression, can you infer that he's really sharing your tale of woe? Or is it a sign of gastritis? Inference from observed behavior is subject to inaccuracy because such inference assumes that only one reality exists: yours. Remember that you will not see the same event in precisely the same way as anyone else. I've already discussed differences due to perception, motivation, expectancies, personal biases, and all the other factors in your phenomenal world. Each of these has an effect on your own observations and inferences.

Sometimes the physical context of observations also promotes inaccuracies. Noise and confusion, for example, can make accurate observation difficult. Physical distance

—being too far away to see or hear the speaker clearly—is another problem. Absence of sensory input affects your perceptions. During the days of the "American Bandstand" television program, a fad among male college students was to turn off the sound and watch the dancers without the musical background. Students found this change in the context titilating as they turned their imaginations loose on the visual stimulus of the sensually gyrating young ladies.

Probably the greatest inaccuracies in inferences from observed behavior stem from permitting our own feelings to get in the way of the other's. That's why I've placed so much emphasis on the need to be aware and in control of our own feelings.

How, then, do you validate inferences? You must first describe to yourself precisely what you observed. "Her jaw is set, and her hands are clenched fists." "He's perspiring, and his breathing is rapid." "He came in and threw his briefcase on the chair." Those statements describe what was observed. Note that they're not judgmental or evaluative. You're not saying that those are good or bad signs or that the other person should or should not behave in that manner. You state only what you see.

Next you must make some kind of inference. "Her jaw is set, and her hands are clenched fists. It appears that she's angry." To check your inference you change the wording slightly and say to the other person, "Your jaw is set, and your hands are clenched fists. Are you angry?" Or "You're perspiring, and your breathing is rapid. Are you anxious about something?"

Note the difference between this approach and the situation in the last chapter where I related my inference that a co-worker was angry and said so without checking. You'll recall his response: "Don't ever tell me how I feel!" If you check your inferences, you let the other person own his feeling. He can share it with you or not as he chooses. You haven't taken it from him and pinned it on him, so to speak. I should have checked my inference with that co-worker. Had I said, "You came in and didn't speak and then slammed your papers on your desk. Are you angry about something?" I wouldn't have added to his anger and become the target of it.

Here's another anecdote which illustrates the types of questions that arise from inferences based on observed behavior:

Chuang Tzu and Hui Tzu were strolling along the dam of the Hao River. Chuang Tzu said, "See how the minnows come out and dart around where they please! That's what fish really enjoy!"

Hui Tzu said, "You're not a fish—how do you know what fish really enjoy?"

Chuang Tzu said, "You're not I, so how do you know I don't know what fish enjoy?"

Hui Tzu said, "I'm not you, so I certainly don't know what you know. On the other hand, you're certainly not a fish—so that still proves that you do not know what fish enjoy!"

Chuang Tzu said, "Let's return to your original question please. You asked me how I knew what fish enjoy—so you already knew I knew it when you asked the question. I know it by standing here beside the Hao."[5]

Real listening, then, is by no means an effortless, passive endeavor. On the contrary, it requires at least as much effort to listen as to speak. And the art of total listening requires much *more* effort than does speaking. It's something like trying to get into the other person's shoes while he's still wearing them.

In summary, there are two basic categories of cues which we can use to figure something about the other's feelings: verbal behaviors and nonverbal behaviors. We must respond to those cues by checking out the accuracy of what we heard or saw. Basing our responses on inferences is too risky because the two types of behavior are often not giving the same message. If there's a question in your mind as to whether the verbal or the nonverbal cues are carrying the message, go with the nonverbal ones, and check out your inferences with the speaker.

Silences are too valuable to destroy. The so-called "pregnant pause" can be used by anyone who really wants to help another gain feeling insights. Silences also help the listener tune in on his own feelings. When silences come, use them to reconstruct what you or the other person just said. Doubtless something that one of you said triggered some deeper feeling.

When you're listening, pay attention first to your facial expression, then to your tone of voice and manner of speaking. What you have to say comes a poor last. A response that merely reflects the speaker's feeling is far better than one which undertakes an in-depth analysis of what he said. Let me caution, however, that accurate reflection of feeling isn't easy. Chapters 13 and 14 will be concerned with that.

In the next chapter we'll look at your response style and see how different kinds of responses affect communications in different ways. You'll experience responding accurately—first to content, later to feelings. In the meantime, here are some things to do:

1. At your first opportunity notice how you customarily handle silence during conversations. If you tend to "jump in," try not to. See what happens when you force the other person to break the silence. Be aware of your own feelings while you try to maintain the silence. Do you feel frustrated? Embarrassed? Anxious? Uncomfortable? Go with the feeling—own it, and you'll find that you can control it. Stay with the here and now.

2. During a conversation, be aware of how you make inferences. What do you use as cues? Do you attend to verbal or nonverbal behaviors? What kinds of inferences do you make?

3. This is another part of exercise 2, but so important that I put it separately. Begin to check out your inferences wherever they come from. State as precisely as you can what you saw—what the other person *did*—then put it into a statement. Ask then if your inference from the behavior you described is correct.
4. Become aware of your own behaviors and what kinds of inferences others make from them.

*Words are like leaves; and where they
most abound, much fruit of sense beneath
is rarely found.*   Alexander Pope

12

Neither Burrowers
Nor Landers Be

I couldn't let this entire book go by without resorting
to the kind of pun for which I'm infamous among my acquaintances. At least these are in a good cause, since they
lead us into a discussion of different kinds of verbal responses and how they affect communication.

Are you a burrower? When someone makes a statement or asks a question, do you follow with a series of
probing questions? Or are you the Ann Landers type who
feels compelled to offer advice? Those are two of a variety
of ways to respond; and each of us, although we may at
times offer alternate responses, has a characteristic style.

Response styles lie at the heart of effective listening.
They can act as facilitators of communication or as inhibitors. Interpersonal communication is a process of give-and-
take. Whenever another person communicates something to
you, the way you respond has the potential to direct the
course of ensuing messages. It can also affect the future
relationship between you and the other person.

Although not all-inclusive, the following is a list of

major response styles we'll be concerned with: (1) advice giving, (2) interpretation, (3) cross-examination, (4) reassurance, and (5) paraphrasing. At times you have probably used the first four, and one or two of them are habitual responses for you. The paraphrasing response, though, is not often used.

As an example of the effect of response on communication, let me share with you an incident at a mental health clinic to which I once referred several parents. As any salesman knows, to be successful you've got to know the territory. That's no less true with regard to working in a mental health clinic. The clinician has to know the territory: the local socioeconomic and cultural factors that may affect the patients concerned. Our new psychologist at this particular clinic neither considered those factors nor bothered to learn that people in the area were not language oriented or sophisticated with regard to therapy. Parents I had referred to this place dropped out of sight after their first contact with this psychologist. When I looked into the matter, I found that they were disappointed with the initial interview. One of them explained it this way: "We went in and sat down, and she just asked us questions and then said, 'I want you to do the talking for the rest of the time you're here.' We didn't know what to say. What good is that? We had some problems that we thought she was going to tell us how to handle."

The moral is that sometimes advice-giving is the right thing—or at least the expedient thing—to do. At times, in fact, each of the five response styles may be appropriate. The goal of communication isn't always the encouragement of openness and sharing; but when it is, your task as a listener is to help the other person understand and become aware of his feelings; and to share those feelings with you to the extent that he wishes to do so. As a listener in those circumstances, you are a helper.

In order to be a good helper, as Egan points out, you need to be perceptive. You need to attend carefully to the other person and hear not only his verbal messages but his nonverbal ones as well. You also need to clarify the other's messages through your interaction with him and, if appropriate, cause him to take action. A good helper is also in touch with his own thoughts and feelings and is aware of how they interact with the feelings and thoughts of the other person. To sum it up, "a good helper is socially intelligent."[1]

Unfortunately, most of us don't act as helpers. We aren't socially intelligent when we need to be—when helping is the goal of the communication. The one response style which best accomplishes that goal is the paraphrase. We should use it if our intention is to help. But what's behind the other response styles? When we use them, what are we trying to prove? What's our intention? Equally important, what is the specific effect of each?

Porter suggests that we do have specific intents for each of the responses we use. We may be making a judgment, playing the part of a teacher, trying to make the other person feel better, directing the other's messages, or checking our perception and clarifying the problem.[2]

Let's take a hypothetical situation and see what kinds of intents are hidden behind each of the five listed response styles (advice-giving, interpretation, cross-examination, reassurance, and paraphrasing); and what happens when each is used.

ADVICE-GIVING. Suppose someone you know approached you and said, "I just don't think I can stand one more day of my supervisor's criticism!" If you respond as an advice-giver, you might say, *"Look, why don't you just tell him off. There's no reason to put up with that kind of thing."*

First, that kind of response is highly judgmental. You're telling your friend that he isn't using good sense or reason and that he's dumb to make such a statement. Advice-giving responses evaluate the speaker and tell him what to do. A response which offers advice has unfortunate consequences for communication. It's the kind of message which often characterizes complementary relationships. It places the listener in a superior position relative to the speaker because it implies that the listener is better able to determine what the situation is and what action should be taken. Like cross-examining responses, advice-giving tends to make the speaker defensive. It also shifts the conversational marble from speaker to listener.

INTERPRETATION. What if your response was an interpretive one? Suppose you replied, for instance, *"You're just saying that because you've been under a lot of pressure at home lately."*

Your intent with that kind of response is to explain to the speaker what his difficulty really is and what and how he should think. This is truly a schizophrenic listener's response because it ignores the speaker's reality and comes from the responder's reality. It implies that you know more about the speaker than he does; you know what causes him to make this statement. The effects of an interpretive response on communication are to shut off openness and sharing because the messages are moved from the feeling level to the cognitive level; they are intellectualized and rationalized. Feelings, remember, are sensual experiences. Because interpretive responses provide information to the speaker regarding his problem, they take away the conversational marble and put the focus on you rather than on him.

CROSS-EXAMINATION. If you offer a cross-examining response, what you intend to do is increase your own knowledge of the speaker's problem, and to clarify it for yourself rather than for him. Like a good trial lawyer, you direct your information-seeking along a particular avenue. This comes close to an "answer yes or no" position and tells the speaker precisely what to talk about. An example of such a response is, *"Exactly what did he say? Has he been like this for a long time?"*

As you can see, that kind of response tends to lead in a different direction from the speaker's intended message.

It pursues the listener's interest instead. In addition to directing the other's messages, the cross-examining response also sets limits on what the other person may talk about.

But although cross-examining responses most often tend to shift the spotlight from feelings to content, they can also be used to clarify feelings. For example, your response to your friend's complaint about her supervisor might be, "I'm not sure I understand; are you angry or are you dejected?"

REASSURANCE. A reassurance response is intended to offer moral support. In reply to your friend's stated problem with her supervisor, you might be inclined to say, "*I wouldn't worry about it; my boss is just like that; always criticizing. I think they're all alike.*"

That's really taking the marble. Although well-intentioned, reassuring responses don't allow the other person to own his own feelings. By trying to "smooth things over," the reassurer implies that the speaker is making too much out of his feelings. Hawaiians have a very good reassuring response which has become an idiom: "Ain't no big thing." The only problem is that, so far as the speaker is concerned, it often *is* a big thing.

Reassurances can have a variety of effects on the course of communications. They can, in addition to minimizing the speaker's feeling, make him feel that you don't realize how serious his problem is; that you don't really understand. The feeling spotlight is again trained on the listener rather than on the speaker. On the positive side, reassuring responses let the speaker know that he's not all alone in the boat, that he's not weird, that others have also had the same feeling.

As previously noted, each of these four response styles may have its place in communications. That is, each can at the appropriate time produce positive effects. But if the purpose of communication is to share feelings, they act for the most part as inhibitors. It is the fifth response style which is necessary for total listening.

PARAPHRASING. When paraphrasing responses are used, the
intention behind them is to find out whether what you
heard is what the speaker wanted you to hear. The paraphrase has some of the characteristics of a cross-examining
response; it seeks information and is intended to clarify.
But unlike cross-examination, the paraphrase seeks information for the speaker's rather than for the respondent's
eventual benefit. It clarifies on the basis of the speaker's
reality, not the respondent's. Paraphrasing responses are
not questions. They are statements that only imply questions. In effect you say to the speaker, "What I understood you to say is this. . . . Did I hear you correctly?"

In response to your friend with the critical boss, you
might paraphrase like this: "*You sound as though you're
really upset with the way things are going at your office.*"
That response lets the other person know that you are sensitive to him at a feeling level. It seeks further information
as to the correctness of your understanding, but it also indicates that you're trying to understand him. It has the
further benefit of helping the speaker understand his own
feelings more clearly and makes him better able to share
them with you. Because paraphrasing responses demonstrate the respondent's caring and acceptance, they encourage the speaker to probe more deeply into his feelings.

We'll work more with paraphrase in chapter 13. Right
now I want to put you to work again. I will provide some
statements. I want you to reply to them by using each of
the response styles covered in this chapter. It's important
that you be able to recognize them when you hear them—
or when you use them.

A. "I can't figure out what's wrong, but lately
I've had a tough time getting up during the
week. On Saturday and Sunday when I
could sleep later, I'm up at the crack of
dawn!"

Respond to this with an example of (1) advice-giving,
(2) interpretation, (3) cross-examination, (4) reassurance,
and (5) paraphrasing. PLEASE WRITE YOUR RESPONSES.

YOU'LL NEED TO REFER TO THEM AGAIN LATER.

Next, do the same with these statements:

B. "I just finished reading that new best seller you recommended. Frankly I thought it was very amateurish. The characters were poorly drawn, and the plot was only so-so. Did you really like it?"

C. "You know, of all the people I've ever met, Joe is the nicest. I don't recall that he has ever said an unkind word about anyone. On the other hand, his wife is a real bitch. I don't know what in the world he ever saw in her."

D. "Remember that opening I said was coming up in my company's home office? Well, what do you think—they asked me if I wanted it. It's a great chance to move up the ladder, but... I don't know, we have so many ties here; our new home, and the kids love the school... I'm not sure how Bill would take it."

Go ahead now and write your five responses to each of those statements. Later you can compare yours with some possible responses listed below. But try not to look at them until you're finished with yours.

Here are some ways you might respond to the four statements in order to demonstrate the five response styles:

A. "I can't figure out what's wrong, but lately I've had a tough time getting up during the week. On Saturday and Sunday when I *could* sleep later, I'm up at the crack of dawn!"

    1. "If I were you, I'd try getting to bed a little earlier during the week and stay up later on Friday and Saturday nights." (Advice-giving.)

2. "The reason you do that is because you're not happy with your job." (Interpretation.)

3. "Didn't you realize when you enrolled in those classes that they would be too heavy a load for you? Why did you take eighteen units in the first place?" (Cross-examination.)

4. "Oh, yeah, I know, I think that's a pretty common thing. It's nothing to be concerned about." (Reassurance.)

5. "It sounds like your everyday responsibilities are getting you down." (Paraphrasing.)

B. "I just finished reading that new bestseller you recommended. Frankly I thought it was very amateurish. The characters were poorly drawn, and the plot was only so-so. Did you really like it?"

1. "You shouldn't have read the book without asking someone else how they liked it. You know how different our tastes are." (Advice-giving.)

2. "It's no wonder you feel that way. You don't care for the author because of the way he conducts his personal life." (Interpretation.)

3. "Why didn't you read the reviews before you read it? Didn't it occur to you that you might not like it?" (Cross-examination.)

4. "Everyone reads a book now and then that he doesn't care for. It isn't a total loss; you can share your disappointment with a lot of other people who didn't like it." (Reassurance.)

5. "You seem puzzled by my recommenda-

tion and disappointed with the quality of the writing." (Paraphrasing.)

C. "You know, of all the people I've ever met, Joe is the nicest. I don't recall that he has ever said an unkind word about anyone. On the other hand, his wife is a real bitch. I don't know what in the world he ever saw in her."

1. "Anyone who feels that way about another person ought to just stay away from her. I'd just ignore Joe's wife and confine my contacts to him." (Advice-giving.)

2. "I think you have that opinion of her right now because she snubbed you at the Smith's party last week." (Interpretation.)

3. "Why don't you just avoid Joe's wife? Why did you insist on going to that party with her when you know the kind of person she is?" (Cross-examination.)

4. "I know how you feel, and you have a lot of company, believe me. None of us likes her." (Reassurance.)

5. "It sounds as if you find it difficult to accept Joe's wife in spite of your admiration of him." (Paraphrasing.)

D. "Remember that opening I said was coming up in my company's home office? Well, what do you think—they asked me if I wanted it. It's a great chance to move up the ladder, but ... I don't know, we have so many ties here; our new home, and the kids love the school. I'm not sure how Bill would take it."

1. "What I'd do is go ahead and take the new job. If you turn it down now you may never get another chance." (Advice-giving.)

2. "What you're really concerned about is how strongly you feel about being a liberated woman. You're afraid that Bill will resent your getting more involved in your work." (Interpretation.)
3. "How could you even consider taking a job that would require you to move? Even though Bill's writing leaves him free to go with you, don't the children come first before a new position?" (Cross-examination.)
4. "These days that kind of a decision is becoming pretty common. Why, my doctor's sister-in-law was in the same situation, and things worked out all right for her. Don't lose any sleep over it." (Reassurance.)
5. "You sound confused about the possible consequences your decision may have with regard to your professional future; but concerned too that if you take the new position your family life may be jeopardized." (Paraphrasing.)

Well, how did you do? Do you think you have a pretty good grasp of the five response styles? Can you recognize each and see what effects each might have on your ability as a listener and helper?

Back at the end of chapter 3 I asked you to write down something and put it in the book for future reference. Well, the future is here. If you will retrieve that paper right now, you'll find that it contains your responses at the beginning of this book to the same four statements you've just seen. Look closely at your response style as it was before you read chapter 12. Are you an advice-giver? An interpreter? A cross-examiner? A reassurer? Or do you have the rare gift of being able to paraphrase naturally?

You might find that your responses are combinations

of response styles—mixed responses. But if you look closely, you'll see that one or two styles are characteristic for you. And if you discovered that your typical response has the effect of shutting off communication, you may want to change your pattern.

Now that you know your characteristic response style, you can decide whether you want to continue with it or shift to one of the others. How open and how able you are to share your feelings will be an important—a deciding—factor in whether you can be comfortable with the paraphrase. Remember the workshop participant who told others in the group, "Anyone who opens up to others these days is crazy!"? Obviously anyone who thinks like that would have difficulty using the paraphrase except on the content level.

In this chapter I discussed five major response styles and how they promote or inhibit the communication of feelings. Of the five, we saw that paraphrasing responses are best to use if the intents are to share feelings and explore them at depth. Paraphrasing responses clearly indicate to the speaker that you're interested in him, not merely in his words.

The next chapter will deal with the paraphrase in detail. We will see that the paraphrase is an empathic response style, that it can deal with either content or feelings. Positive and negative kinds of response will be discussed, and we will learn what the paraphrase is and is not.

Before we leave chapter 12, I want to give you one more assignment. Although you can get some shadow of response styles and their effects from the written exercises, in order to get the substance you need to actually try them out. You also need to get an idea of how you react when others respond to your statements with each of the styles.

How many times have you disallowed another person his feelings with such responses as "there, it's nothing to worry about," "don't cry," or "I know just how you feel" without realizing what you were doing? Supportive responses are the most popular.

Here, then, are four things I'd like you to do:

1. Make a list of a dozen or so responses of different styles that others make to your statements, and be aware of how you react to each of them. Which style of response makes you feel best? Worst?

2. Make a list of a dozen or so responses that you make to others' statements. Examine these responses; which ones do you use most? Be aware of how others react to your responses.

3. Substitute paraphrase for your characteristic style, and see whether the reaction is different from what you usually get. Try this with a dozen or so statements. Do you like the effect better?

4. Select two or three people you like best or who are the most popular people of your acquaintance. What is their characteristic response style?

"Who are you, aged man?" I said,
"And how is it you live?"
And his answer trickled through my head
Like water through a sieve   Lewis Carroll

13

The Response-Ability
Is All Yours

This is a key chapter. As you begin reading it, there are some things you'll want to keep in mind regarding your responsibility as a listener. To start with, remember where the conversational marble belongs. Your point of view isn't what counts; it's the other person you should focus on. That doesn't mean that your feelings should be ignored; by no means. When the process of understanding requires it, as we have seen, you need to share your feelings. At all times, of course, you need to be aware of them.

By this time you know that inferences are chancy and that it's hazardous to assume that you've correctly understood what the other person intended you to know. It's necessary to check your perceptions and your understandings. And paraphrase is the best way to do that, unless you happen to be a clairvoyant. Remember, then, to be aware of your feelings, to share them when necessary, and to check with the other person to make sure you heard him correctly. Above all, try to keep the focus of attention on the other.

With those words of reminder, let's consider some

other words. We want to find out what's involved in getting into the other person's feelings and how to make him aware of this. We'll need to know two key words.

One day this past week I picked up an antiquated, well-thumbed edition of *Webster's Collegiate Dictionary.* Pure chance—and the fact that I was looking for it— caused me to open the book to the page where the word *empathy* should have appeared. It wasn't there. But I finally located it at the front of the dictionary in the new words section. I ruminated about that word, *empathy,* and the fact that it was a new word "way back there in the olden days," as my kids refer to my childhood years. And it occurred to me that empathy, to many of us, is still a new—and strange—word.

For most of us, empathizing takes a good bit of practice, although some people seem to be born with the gift. When the ability to empathize isn't a natural or seemingly natural attribute, people often involve themselves in training groups whose stated goal is to acquire it. That's one way to do it. But it's possible to become a reasonably skilled empathizer without entering the training group kind of experience. Acquiring the skill really should be considered an obligation because, along with love, what the world needs now is empathy. There's a real shortage.

In addition to words, I am interested in cause-and-effect relationships. So I ruminated about why more people —more homes, more offices, more schools, more classrooms —seem to lack that empathic quality than seem to have it. I decided that we psychologists, counselors, and others in the "helping professions" are to blame, at least in part. We've adopted the word—if not always the practice—and have somehow become very proprietary about its use. But neither the word nor its spirit is, or should be, anyone's private property. Therefore I, for one, hereby bestow upon you rights and privileges equal to mine for use of empathy.

You'll find that empathy is defined in your dictionary as something like "the projecting of one's self into the situation of another person, and the undergoing of sensations believed to be associated with that situation." That's a fancy way of saying that empathy is feeling what it's like to wear the other fellow's shoes.

In my workshops I find that most people do possess the qualities requisite to the exercise of empathy but that they keep them latent—submerged—and don't permit them to surface. I find too that it's much easier for most of us to be empathic with strangers and casual acquaintances than with those who are close to us. I recall, for instance, a family I counseled.

The parents were infuriated with their teen-aged son's disregard for their feelings and his lack of consideration. Knowing how he behaved at home, they were continually astounded when people who had come in contact with him told them what a fine, polite, considerate, and helpful boy he was. Finally the exasperated father reportedly said, "Son, would you please do your mother and me a favor? Stop treating us as if we were your parents. Make believe we're strangers."

I don't recall whether the boy exhibited any remarkable behavior change in response to his father's plea; but I do recall that, during the course of counseling sessions, both parents began to realize that they had never given their son the empathy they were seeking from him. If we can believe that children display those attributes of character which their parents model for them as they grow up, it's no wonder that this young man behaved as he did toward his parents. The only empathy he received came from friends and acquaintances. The lessons, I suppose, are that empathy is not something you ask for—it's something you give; and that like charity, empathy should begin at home. Unfortunately in our society love, openness, and sharing are not practiced at home, and so disclosing one's self and sharing feelings is more often easier with strangers than with loved ones.

Another reason why those most in need of empathy

from people close to them are denied it is that they often behave in a manner that discourages the giving of it. I've already talked about the ways in which home and school contribute to poor listening habits, but not only listening habits are neglected. For example, a child who comes to school from a home where the day began with a shouting match between mother and father certainly needs empathy; but he's more likely to receive punishment than empathy from his teacher. If he's frightened and acts out the accompanying feelings of aggression, he discourages the thing he most needs, because aggressive behavior is unpleasant, and the teacher doesn't want to get involved with it. We're all ready and willing to project ourselves into pleasant situations, but it's another story, if the situation is unpleasant. Suppose a friend informs you that his ticket on the Irish Sweepstakes just won him a hundred thousand dollars. It's easy to hurl yourself headlong into empathic frenzy over that bit of fortune. But that kind of immersion into the other's situation isn't quite so easy when a neighbor tells you that the landlord just raised his rent to the point where moving has become necessary. Similarly it's easy to be empathic when Betsy gets all "A's" on her final examinations, but not so easy when Billy brings home a report card on which the highest grade is "F."

It's simple to identify people who lack the ability to empathize or don't. Often the giveaway is their impatience. In my work with schools, for example, I frequently encounter teachers who are impatient with slow-learning children. Sad to say, I generally find that the parents of these same children are also impatient with them. Unless we begin serving as empathic models for our children, we'll raise another generation of unempathic adults who are experts, as Egan put it, at "hiding out from themselves and others."[1] When we consider the average little Fig Newton over there in the second row, we tend to forget that what now comes so easily to us as adults may not have come so readily when we were little Miss Fig Newton's age. Acquisition of language skills, for example, may not come as easily as we think it should to our offspring.

The empathic person is sufficiently involved in feelings to identify with a child and understand the problems of learning as a child experiences them. For most of us that isn't easy to do, because we have the happy faculty of forgetting the difficult, painful, and unpleasant.

Have you ever tried to recall the process by which you first learned to read? If not, try it for the mental exercise if nothing else. Even if you don't succeed in remembering, you'll be forced to give some thought to the possibility that you too had difficulties as a student at an early age. This awareness will sharpen up your empathic mode toward your children and toward other adults who may not read as well as they would like.

One thing we may now be able to appreciate is the pressure inherent in being under someone's evaluative eye for four or five hours every day, five days per week, nine months per year. Is it any wonder that, for some kids, recesses, lunch period, and dismissal are the only bright spots in the school day? Imagine your boss looking over your shoulder all day. Imagine also your feelings at being tested and graded at regular intervals by your boss; and further, think how you'd like it if your grade on job performance had to be taken home for your family's examination and signature. That's an exercise that should generate some empathy!

An assistant school superintendent and I were discussing learning, teachers, and people in general and their feelings. He said, "I believe that in order for children to learn, they have to be frustrated. It's the motivation that the desire to relieve the frustration produces that results in learning." That educator was empathic, aware that learning involves frustration.

I thought of my experience in taking a course in intensive Spanish. The process is called "total immersion," one that many of you may have experienced. It's hard to describe the way tension builds up when you're required to use a strange language for extended periods of time; you feel utter frustration when you can't find the correct word or proper tense of a verb or when the pronunciation just doesn't come. That's the kind of recollection that will make you empathic toward others—especially toward school children trying to learn strange new ways of dealing with language under conditions completely foreign to their out-of-school existence. A fellow psychologist once remarked that without realizing it, we have made children the largest slave labor force in the history of the world.

But not only school children are asked to perform daily drudgery without recompense. See if you can empathize with anyone in the following analogy. You're a homemaker, and your housecleaning chores are finished for the day. It's late afternoon. You're preparing dinner when your husband arrives home from the office as is usual every day at this time. He circuits the living room, then goes through each bedroom in turn. Ten minutes later he comes into the kitchen; and again, as customary every day at this time, he seats himself at the table, examining it and the rest of the room as he does so, places a sheet of paper on the table, and begins making notes. Finally he rises, walks toward you, and for the first time acknowledges your presence:

"Here's your report card for today, dear. The living room looks much better today; so do the bathroom and spare bedroom. But you still seem to be having trouble getting our bedroom the way I want it. I'm sorry but I had to give you another bad report because of that and because the bed still isn't made the way I told you to do it."

"I'm sorry, dear," you reply, "I know how particular you are about the way the bed is made and I do try, but..."

"But what? I spent an hour last week showing you how to do it. There's nothing difficult about it."

"Yes, I know you showed me, but I still don't get it."

"Oh, come on now, it's very simple. I can't believe you when you say you're really trying to do it right. I'll just have to keep giving you failing reports until you begin to apply yourself. Don't forget to take your report card to the dinner table tonight so that the children can look at it. Maybe they can get you to try harder. Apparently I can't. Oh, and don't forget to have them sign it, too."

That may sound ludicrous, but there are millions of women whose husbands unconsciously treat them just that way. There's no understanding of how it feels to perform what many wives consider to be dull, uninteresting chores day after day without any kind of payoff. Husbands of other, more fortunate millions at least acknowledge that their wives have provided a pleasant home environment, assumed the major responsibility for the children's welfare, and prepare taste-tempting meals. For men and working women, the problem isn't quite so bad. At least they're given monetary reinforcement, and often they receive secondary kinds of reinforcement as well.

As adults we perform the tasks required by our occupations for two kinds of pay. For men and the many women with business careers, there is first of all the wage or salary received. It's fair to say that few if any of us would continue to report at our work stations for long if we ceased to receive a paycheck.

But beyond the paycheck are secondary reinforcers; those which deal with feelings and are social in nature, like recognition, approval, promotion, praise, acceptance, and love. And these too are essential because they indicate that feelings are an important consideration in job satisfaction —and because without them we wouldn't be motivated to bring any quality or improvement to the work we do. I have known employers who managed to maintain a high standard of production and keep their employees despite the fact that their pay scales were substantially lower than those of their competitors. Because they were empathic, they knew the importance of giving recognition and praise when they couldn't afford pay increases.

Governor Edmund G. Brown, Jr., of California expressed the same kind of philosophy with regard to top-ranking employees of the state. He believed that pay for jobs that are interesting and complex should be lower than pay for jobs which are routine and unchallenging. Whether or not you agree with the governor's idea, it does at least recognize the fact that the employee invests an element of feeling in his work, and that if the employer responds to that investment with empathy, he provides a meaningful payoff.

Now let's look more closely at several things which indicate whether or not the listener is an empathic person. We'll also consider the second word which shares the focus of this chapter: "paraphrase."

The poorest way to respond to another person is to ignore what he said. I think that the worst hurt anyone can suffer is to reach out, share a deep feeling, and get no response. That's a complete denial of the sharer as a person. As noted earlier, even a pure content response is better than no response at all. So let's try to avoid the nonresponse.

Content responses can be of various kinds and can have a variety of effects. One response which provides discomfort is the judgmental type in which the listener keeps the marble at all times. A characteristic expression is "I'll buy that." There's no attempt to respond beyond the surface content level, and the effect is to patronize the listener, to place the responder in a superior position to the speaker.

Another response, judgmental and evaluative, is the negative of the one just mentioned: "I don't buy that." This is also argumentative and limits the conversation to content, shutting out feelings which stay locked up inside the communicators. Again, the speaker is put in an inferior position relative to the listener. The implication is that the speaker is obliged to prove the accuracy of what he has said.

A third kind of response is an outright rejection of whatever the speaker said. Unlike either of the above kinds, this is not an argumentative reply. It completely cuts off any further communication. It might be done by turning one's back on the speaker or by leaving the room. In either case, there's no reply even though there is implicit acknowledgment that the speaker's words were heard.

Another kind of response to content is frequently practiced. Many people habitually assume that they know exactly what you're going to say, and they seem to delight in trying to finish your sentences for you. Often they're incorrect, and the conversation bogs down as you try to straighten the error and get back on the track. A variation of this kind of response is when the listener interprets for you the content of your message. A typical response of this type begins "In other words . . ." Then there's the kind of response mentioned before, in which the listener seizes upon some fact or statistic in your statement and runs with it, taking your content along with him but leaving your feelings behind.

As I said, these are poor kinds of response. They are negatively oriented and will never get beyond the content level of communication. Not even the lowest level of empathy can sneak in. Still, these are better than no response at all.

Positive kinds of response include some sort of expression that the listener agrees with what he heard—a nod of the head, an affirmative word, or a simple "Uh huh"—any of these will cause the speaker to continue because they indicate that his words have fallen on fertile ground. But head-nodding and "Uh huh" don't indicate that feelings have been communicated, and so are not empathic responses.

A second kind of positive response seeks further information. If a student says to a professor "I don't like classes in which the students have to do all the work," the professor might seek clarification: "Are you saying that you think I'm not doing enough in this class?" That would let the student know that his message has been heard but not understood. It may also mean that the professor is defensive and takes exception to the remark. Because he's dependent on the professor for his grade, the student, also defensive, may elect to end the conversation at that point if the professor doesn't. This too falls far short of empathy.

The best kind of response is the one which lets the speaker know that his message has been heard, understood, and accepted without judgment or evaluation. It encourages the speaker to share more of himself with the listener. This kind of response is called "paraphrase," and it includes the variety of empathic responses.

We discussed the paraphrase briefly in chapter 12, but now let's examine it in detail. First of all, what is paraphrase? When we paraphrase, we may simply restate what we heard the speaker say, so that we can check our perception and also let the speaker know his words were heard. "This place always reminds me of home" might be paraphrased as "you always think of home when you're here." That's a low-level paraphrase, reflecting only the content of what the speaker said.

At the highest level, the paraphrase can be used to bring to the surface feelings which the speaker may be unaware of or concealing. In between are other levels at which the willingly shared feelings of the speaker are reflected, and he is thus encouraged to explore and share deeper feeling. Higher level paraphrase proceeds from observing that the important thing is not the words of the speaker but what makes him say them. It can't happen if we sit in judgment of his words; it can't happen if we try to show that we're mind readers; and it can't happen if every conversation is controlled by the listener. It certainly won't happen if your interest in the speaker's words is forced and you use the paraphrase as a tool to trick him into revealing his feelings. Your interest has to be real.

A reasonable question at this point is, what is the value of paraphrase? For the answer, we must return to the matter of differing realities—to the definition of schizophrenic listening. We've noted that each of us sees and hears things in the light of our own heredity, nurturance, education, self-concept, and motivation. We also know that we tend to think that everyone else perceives the same situation just as we do and that words have universal meanings. We've seen that all these factors impinge on our understanding of what others say. The only way we can seek to overcome the communication difficulties resulting from them is to check back with the person who spoke the words.

Communication may be thought of as a three-step, circular process. At step one the speaker should communicate his message concretely enough to be clear and to describe his thinking and feelings accurately at the moment. Step two requires that the listener then provide feedback —a response that lets the speaker know how his message was received and understood by the listener. In step three the speaker verbally affirms or denies the accuracy of the listener's feedback. Paraphrase is simply the most effective kind of feedback.

Participants in my workshops almost always feel uncomfortable when they begin to experience use of the paraphrase. One reason, I imagine, is that each of us has been programmed to hide and be uncomfortable with certain feelings; consequently we don't find it easy to explore those same feelings in others. Nor is it pleasant at first to have others explore them in us when we know they're doing it. That unpleasant sensation vanishes when we see that others are accepting of our "forbidden" feelings.

Another problem is that paraphrase is frequently first

used in a manipulative fashion. When others sense the lack of real caring, they become uneasy (and perhaps angry). In one workshop a group member with some training in psychology fancied herself as quite skillful in analyzing the behavior of others. After about the fifth meeting, two of the participants came to me to complain about the amateur analyst. They said they resented the fact that she didn't really participate in the experiential activities. "She tries to give the impression that she's really taking part, but she just kind of sits back and studies the rest of us while we're spilling out our guts. We feel like we're being examined under a microscope."

Another uncomfortable feeling in using paraphrase concerns the listener's belief that nothing can happen when all he does is repeat what the speaker says. Don't be fooled. Being listened to is such a rare experience that *any* indication of being heard will literally turn the speaker on to the listener. The results of paraphrase are immediately obvious if the listener attends to the speaker rather than to how he as listener feels about using paraphrase. When it's genuine, paraphrasing is both comfortable and comforting.

Our habits as communicators must completely change when we begin to use paraphrase. We're accustomed when we converse with others to tell them what we know about the subject at hand. We're conditioned to think that we must demonstrate knowledgeability on the topic or others will think we're uninformed or stupid. Truth is, when you tell another what he already knows, he's amazed at how clever you are. He might respond, "You took the words right out of my mouth." A wag once remarked that it's better to keep your mouth shut and have others think you a fool than to open it and remove all doubt. Notwithstanding that, each of us has a need to tell others about things we know; and if paraphrase is properly used, the other person, having been fully heard, should finally want to hear what you have to say. If he doesn't, then he's someone you'll not often seek to converse with. You'll find someone able to paraphrase your words and feelings in return, someone who wants to learn from you.

Now let's try some sample paraphrases: on the first level, a simple restatement of facts. We've already seen one example:

> "This place always reminds me of home."
> "You always think of home when you're here."

Here's another:

> "You can't imagine how different everything looks to me now."
> "You're seeing things in a different light these days."

At a slightly higher level, feelings are included in the paraphrase along with the content, and empathy enters the verbal interchange:

> "Anytime I get a class like this I'm bored with it."
> "You seem to be disappointed that you took this class, and you find it dull."

The last sentence reflects the feeling that you heard the speaker describe. Next comes the response which paraphrases the expressed feeling rather than the described one or, in other words, responds to the nonverbal language of the speaker and the feelings implied by his words.

> "I don't know where those people at the office expect me to get enough time to do everything they're asking me to do. I'm working my tail off, and all they do is criticize!"
> "Sounds like you feel resentful about having too much of a load and worried that you won't get everything done on time. It really hurts that others are so unappreciative of what you do."

Get the idea? The speaker didn't describe his feelings, but the listener attended to the nonverbal cues behind the words as well as to the words themselves and was able to paraphrase the feelings. At this point the speaker will either say, "Yes, dammit, there's just no appreciation for

all I do. I wish I could just tell all of them to go to hell!";
or "well, not exactly. I do resent having such a load all
right, but I know I'll get it done on schedule. It's just that
I wish they'd recognize my contribution!" In any case the
conversation is off and running, and the speaker will feel
warm and comfortable knowing that the listener is genuinely interested.

Now I'm going to give you a statement. I want you to
respond to it on the three levels presented in this chapter.
First respond to the content—the words alone; then to the
feelings you hear described; and finally to the nonverbal
or implied feelings.

> "I hate the end of the year. All it means is Christ-
> mas and more expenses. And on top of everything
> else, I just got my property tax bill and the income
> tax forms in today's mail. I'm fed up with paying
> the big salaries of all the crooked politicians who
> run this country!"

Go ahead, see what you can do to get into that unfortunate person's feelings. If you happen to be a politician,
be careful that your own feelings don't get in the way—but
do be aware of them.

Here are some possible responses; you may have better ones. The main thing is for you to see that paraphrase
can exist on different response levels.

1. Responding to content: "You don't like the
   end of the year because of the heavy financial
   burden it means, and you think the merchants,
   the government, and the politicians are to
   blame."
2. Responding to described feelings: "Sounds as
   though you're fed up with the holiday season
   and the end of the year expenses. You're under
   a lot of pressure because of seasonal bills and
   feel like you're being taken advantage of by
   the government and commercial interests."

3. Responding to implied feelings: "You seem
    disgusted with the holiday season. No matter
    where you turn you're being ripped off. If it
    isn't the merchants, it's the government. I'll
    bet you'd just like to escape to some quiet
    place and forget all the hassle."

In this chapter we looked in detail at empathy and
the paraphrase. We also tried on some content and empathic paraphrases for size. In chapter 14 we'll work further
with empathic paraphrase and find out how to form the
different levels of empathic paraphrase.

As a closing assignment, please do the following:

1. Practice using paraphrase as a response to
    feelings as often as you can. Observe the re-
    sults closely.

2. Keeping aware of your own feelings, try using
    paraphrase of feelings in an emotional situa-
    tion. If someone becomes angry, for example,
    see what happens if you respond to the anger
    rather than to the words (e.g., "Something
    seems to have made you very angry"). Simi-
    larly if someone is very happy or elated, re-
    spond to the happiness or elation and observe
    what happens to the other person—and to
    yourself.

3. Remember what we learned about silence.
    Your paraphrase may be followed by silence.
    Use that silence. Your paraphrase may have
    caused the speaker to become aware of a feel-
    ing he was previously unaware of. Let him
    explore that feeling in peace. When he's ready,
    he'll share more of his feelings if he believes
    you are really with him.

If you explain something so clearly that
no one can misunderstand, someone will.   Chisholm's Third Law

14

A Little
Lily-Gilding:
Total Listening

If you've been paying attention up to this point, you've pretty thoroughly examined the problem of schizophrenic listening, how it begins and develops. If you've actively involved yourself in the suggested exercises and assignments, you have also had a look into yourself as a feeling individual. You've obtained a fairly good idea (depending on the degree to which you permitted yourself) of the limitations you put on your own freedom to feel—to respond to your own emotions—and to be. To the extent that you were willing to try, you now have a knowledge of how your feelings about yourself and others determine the way that you respond: your response style. You also know the expected effect of your response style on your ability to communicate with others and on the ability of others to communicate with you. You've taken a first look at the difference between responses aimed at the content—words —of messages and responses aimed at the feelings behind those words. You have practiced using the paraphrasing response and were introduced to the kind of paraphrasing response called the empathic response, or empathy.

In this chapter we'll bring it all together. We'll pursue the matter of the empathic response and develop it more fully. Your skill in using the empathic response is the key to a deeper understanding of the often concealed or misunderstood messages of others. As that understanding deepens, you'll also deepen your understanding of yourself.

That different depths of empathic response exist is universally agreed. Not a matter of universal agreement among those who have studied the question is precisely how many levels there are. Carkhuff and Berenson listed five levels of "empathic understanding."[1]

At the lowest step in their hierarchy is the kind of response which indicates that the words have been heard, but there is no awareness of feelings. Suppose someone were to say to you "wow, it sure is hot today. I don't feel like doing a thing!" At the lowest level your response might be "yeah, it's hot, all right."

The second level is a response to your own feelings as a listener, but not to the speaker's. Using the same statement "wow, it sure is hot etc.," the second level of empathic response could be something like "I'm completely sapped. I think I'll try to find a cool spot and just collapse."

A third-level empathic response a la Carkhuff and Berenson indicates an accurate understanding of surface feelings but not of deeper feelings. "Sounds like you don't care for hot weather." The speaker's feeling of discomfort is paraphrased, but a lot is left out.

On the fourth level the listener responds to the speaker's feelings at a deeper feeling level than the other person was able to express. A possible response might be "hot weather seems to make you really uncomfortable and not much inclined to expend any energy."

A fifth-level empathic response shows that the listener is really tuned in on the speaker's wavelength: "This heat has really got you down. You feel as though every ounce of energy has been drawn out of you, and you'd just like to find a cool, shady spot and not have to lift a finger."

As you can see, that last response goes far beyond a mere basic understanding of what was explicitly stated by the speaker. It gets at the implicit message. It lets the speaker know you have really heard what he was feeling and that you are "with him."

Another specialist in the art of helping lists six levels of empathy. Egan has developed a scale with levels of communication labeled "very poor," "poor," "inadequate," "adequate," "good," and "very good."[2] Let's look at each of these kinds of response as related to the following statement:

"Boss, I can't believe that I'm imagining things. I have the feeling that you've been avoiding me for the past few days. Perhaps it isn't avoidance I sense; maybe it's more like I feel you're cutting me out, trying to get rid of me. I don't know how to handle it."

A "very poor" response to that statement would be "Jones, I'm busy. Why don't you talk to me some other time?" That kind of response, whether or not the boss is trying to get rid of Jones, would serve to alienate him, make him even more uncomfortable and certain that he's on his way out.

A response which falls into the "poor" classification: "You might try talking to Smithers about this. He seems to have the same feeling." There's no understanding shown on the part of the boss; instead, he offers Jones advice.

Next up the ladder is the "inadequate" response: something like "is that so?" This communicates nothing because it's too vague—lacks concreteness—and doesn't address itself to the concerns expressed by Jones.

An "adequate" response indicates at least minimal recognition of the speaker's feelings. Jones' boss would give him an adequate response if he said, "You're really disturbed by this, aren't you?" But there is still no indication that the boss is aware of, or interested in, the reasons why Jones is disturbed. This is a surface response.

Here is what Egan might consider a "good" response:

"You feel that there's a distance between us that wasn't there before, and that's really bothering you." In that response is recognition of both the feeling and the reason underlying the feeling.

At the top of the empathy ladder is the "very good" response which could be something such as "You feel that I'm avoiding you and that my avoidance means that I'm pushing you out, trying to get rid of you. That hurts you because you've felt close to me, and it disturbs you because you feel insecure about your job. You feel helpless because you don't know what to do about all this."

Tubesing and Tubesing simplified the Carkhuff and Berenson classification of empathic responses to four instead of five response types by combining levels four and five. These proceed, as before, from paraphrase of content to the paraphrase which adds to the speaker's understanding of his own feelings.[3]

As in other classifications, the lowest or first-level empathic response completely ignores the feelings implicit in the speakers's message and may even subtract from the content. First-level responses are those related to advice-giving, interpretation, cross-examination, or reassurance—the response styles discussed in chapter 12. They are argumentative, judgmental, and evaluative. At worst they serve as denial of the other person.

Second-level empathic responses also ignore the feelings implicit in the speaker's communication but do, at least, accurately respond to the content. They don't deny the speaker, but they do deny his feelings. Second-level empathic responses may be of the advice-giving, interpretive, or reassuring type.

Third-level empathic responses begin to approach the feeling behind the speaker's communication. They attend to the content and reflect the most obvious feelings—generally those expressed verbally and those actually described by the speaker. But nothing in this response would serve to deepen the speaker's understanding of what is making him speak.

The fourth level of empathic response is the real helping response. Such responses show that the listener is paying attention to the content of the speaker's communication and that he is also in touch with the speaker's feelings. The listener tunes in to the verbal and nonverbal language of the speaker, and his responses go beyond the speaker's understanding of his own feelings and emotions and help him gain a deeper insight.

Here are some examples which illustrate these four levels of empathic response to a statement:

STATEMENT: "It's hard to explain, but lately I've had the strangest feeling—like something's going to happen to me; something terrible. I wake up in the middle of the night, and I'm all sweaty; my heart pounds, and I'm just plain scared. Am I going nuts or something?"

FIRST-LEVEL RESPONSE: "I don't know but if I were you, I'd go to the doctor about that waking up. Maybe he can give you something."

SECOND-LEVEL RESPONSE: "I think you're scared for no good reason. It's probably only a nightmare."

THIRD-LEVEL RESPONSE: "This business of being afraid for no reason you can put your finger on seems to be really disturbing you. You're sure it isn't normal."

FOURTH-LEVEL RESPONSE: "It sounds as though you're very anxious about something that isn't clear to you. The fact that you can't pinpoint your feelings of fear makes you even more anxious—so much so that you've begun losing sleep and having other physical symptoms. Because you can't seem to find a real reason for all this, you're beginning to wonder about your mental health, and you don't know what to do about it."

Those are only some possible responses, of course, but they will give you guidelines for forming your own responses. Let's go through the process again with another statement:

STATEMENT: "You know, I really like Elaine, but yesterday when I overheard her criticizing me in that restaurant, it really burned me up. Maybe she was right and I deserved the criticism, but still . . . I mean, why couldn't she have told *me*? I thought she was my friend, but friends don't talk to others about you that way, do they?"

FIRST-LEVEL RESPONSE: "I'm ready for another drink; how about you?"

SECOND-LEVEL RESPONSE: "I don't think you should let that bother you. I know Elaine made you mad, but that's the way she is."

THIRD-LEVEL RESPONSE: "You're really angry with Elaine for talking about you behind your back, and you don't think she's a very good friend."

FOURTH-LEVEL RESPONSE: "It sounds like Elaine really hurt you when she told others something about you that should have been a confidential matter between friends. The fact that she chose to reveal it to others makes you feel betrayed by someone you trusted, and that makes you angry."

You've probably got the idea now, but let's go through it just once more. Here's another statement:

STATEMENT: "Well, of all the nerve! We've been standing in this line for at least half an hour waiting to buy tickets, and that guy just pushed his way to the head of the line. I'd like to know what makes him think he's somebody special. If we can wait, so can he. And what's the matter with that cashier, letting him do it? I'll bet he's a friend of hers. Somebody should have told her off—both of them!"

FIRST-LEVEL RESPONSE: "Yeah. Say, what time is it, anyway?"

SECOND-LEVEL RESPONSE: "I don't like waiting either, but I guess we're all in the same boat."

THIRD-LEVEL RESPONSE: "Sounds like people who want preferential treatment make you angry; especially when they get by with it."

FOURTH-LEVEL RESPONSE: "It sounds as though fairness is very important to you. You're infuriated when someone takes unfair advantage. What's even more infuriating is your feeling of helplessness when you see that there's nothing you can do about it."

Now the whole picture should be completely clear, Chisholm's Third Law notwithstanding. How about trying your wings? On the chalkboard in a school office I once saw the words "You can fly, but first you've got to get rid of that cocoon." Well, you've spent lots of time, energy, and thought on getting rid of that cocoon, that ball of feelings in which you've been encased all these years. Now it's time for you to fly.

Here are some communications for you to paraphrase at the four levels of empathy:

A.   "Boy, if there's one thing I hate, it's having to present a term paper to that class. I've never seen such a critical bunch!"

B.   "Maybe it's just my imagination, but Helen seemed distant the other night. I tried to talk with her, but I had the feeling she just wasn't interested. It bothered me, because that just isn't like her."

C.   "You know, I don't mind people pointing out my errors if the purpose is to improve things —to correct the process. But with Oscar it's a matter of finding fault for the sake of finding fault. I've about had it with his nit-picking!"

D.   "I'm beginning to get worried about all the things I have to do. There just doesn't seem to be enough hours in the day. I've got a deadline to meet for that class I'm teaching, and I don't think I'll make it. I really feel boxed in."

E.   "That was a great conference, the best I've ever attended. There were so many new techniques presented that have such promise. I'm anxious to try them out in my own practice. And Bill Smith's keynote speech was out-

standing. What he had to say should have
been said a long time ago!"

All right, there you have five statements with a variety of feelings implied. See what you can do with each of
them. Start with first-level responses, and build up to the
fourth level. I have provided some responses with which
you can check, but as usual, don't refer to them until you've
attempted your own responses.

Here are possible responses to the five statements:

STATEMENT A: "Boy, if there's one thing I hate, it's
having to present a term paper to that class. I've never
seen such a critical bunch!"

FIRST-LEVEL RESPONSE: "Say, speaking of class, I've
got to run or I'll be late." (Ignores almost all of content
and ignores all of the feelings.)

SECOND-LEVEL RESPONSE: "Presenting term papers
isn't really all that bad." (Attends to content but denies
feelings.)

THIRD-LEVEL RESPONSE: "Sounds like that bunch is so
critical that you're apprehensive about presenting your
paper." (Attends to content and surface feelings.)

FOURTH-LEVEL RESPONSE: "It sounds to me as though
you're reluctant to share your ideas with a group of people
you think won't accept them. They're so critical that
you're afraid they'll just take the opportunity to humiliate
you, and that makes you feel apprehensive." (Responds
to both content and deeper feelings.)

STATEMENT B: "Maybe it's just my imagination, but
Helen seemed distant the other night. I tried to talk with
her, but I had the feeling she just wasn't interested. It
bothered me, because that just isn't like her."

FIRST-LEVEL RESPONSE: "Oh, I don't think it was anything. She was like that with everybody." (Denies content
and feelings.)

SECOND-LEVEL RESPONSE: "You think that Helen ignored you the other night, but that shouldn't concern you; she was probably just not feeling well." (Responds to content but judges the feelings.)

THIRD-LEVEL RESPONSE: "When Helen seemed turned off to you the other night, you were concerned about the sudden change." (Responds to content and surface feelings.)

FOURTH-LEVEL RESPONSE: "It sounds like Helen's seeming disinterest in what you had to say has you puzzled. You feel estranged from her, and that's a new and very uncomfortable sensation. You're wondering if Helen wants to end your relationship, and that makes you feel perplexed and a bit dejected." (Responds to content and deeper feelings, adding to the expressed feelings.)

STATEMENT C: "You know, I don't mind people pointing out my errors if the purpose is to improve things—to correct the process. But with Oscar it's a matter of finding fault for the sake of finding fault. I've about had it with his nit-picking!"

FIRST-LEVEL RESPONSE: "Don't let it bother you. Everybody hates his guts." (Denial of both content and feelings.)

SECOND-LEVEL RESPONSE: "Oscar seems to have gotten to you, but you shouldn't pay any attention to him." (Responds to content, makes judgment about feelings.)

THIRD-LEVEL RESPONSE: "When Oscar is critical of your work, you think he's doing it just to bug you, and that annoys you." (Responds to content and surface feelings.)

FOURTH-LEVEL RESPONSE: "It seems to me that you're saying that Oscar's criticism is destructive and directed at you rather than at your work. That kind of thing makes you angry. If he'd only suggest a better way, you could do something with that, but his constant and useless fault-finding is something that frustrates you because you can't deal with it." (Responds to content and gives the speaker a deeper understanding of his feelings.)

STATEMENT D: "I'm beginning to get worried about all the things I have to do. There just doesn't seem to be enough hours in the day. I've got a deadline to meet for that class I'm teaching, and I don't think I'll make it. I really feel boxed in."

FIRST-LEVEL RESPONSE: "Why don't you take some time off and go fishing?"

SECOND-LEVEL RESPONSE: "You're under a lot of pressure, but don't worry; things will work out."

THIRD-LEVEL RESPONSE: "With all the work you have to get done you're beginning to get a little panicky."

FOURTH-LEVEL RESPONSE: "There are so many things facing you right now that even the thought exhausts you. You feel responsible for your new class, and your preparations for it have just added to your burden. All of this makes you feel that you're trapped and there's no way out."

STATEMENT E: "That was a great conference, the best I've ever attended. There were so many new techniques presented that have such promise. I'm anxious to try them out in my own practice. And Bill Smith's keynote speech was outstanding. What he had to say should have been said a long time ago!"

FIRST-LEVEL RESPONSE: "I'm glad it's over. I don't think I could have sat on that hard chair for another minute."

SECOND-LEVEL RESPONSE: "Bill Smith was good all right, and there were some interesting ideas presented, but I don't think the conference was all that exciting."

THIRD-LEVEL RESPONSE: "That whole conference really turned you on. New ways of doing your work are exciting to you. Bill Smith has your enthusiastic support because he said something you've been aware of for some time.

You're pleased that others see the need to do something about it."

FOURTH-LEVEL RESPONSE: I'm going to let you puzzle over a fourth-level empathic response to statement E because I want to deal with it in the final chapter.

To conclude this chapter, I want to summarize the four levels of empathic response. This is your last chance to get them sorted out, and it's important that you be able to recognize the differences.

First-level responses: No attention is paid to either the content of the speaker's communication or his feelings. The listener may completely ignore, deny, argue with, or evaluate what the speaker has said.

Second-level responses: The listener attends to the content of the speaker's communication, but he may completely ignore, deny, or evaluate the feelings implied or expressed by the speaker.

Third-level responses: The listener attends to both content and feelings of the speaker's communication; but the response is only to the verbal language and surface feelings, not to the deeper feelings and nonverbal component of the speaker's communication.

Fourth-level responses: In this truly empathic response, the listener replies to verbal and nonverbal language.

And there you have it. That, as we sometimes say, is "the whole ball of wax." If you can use the four levels of empathic response, you have a powerful tool for helping others come to a better understanding of themselves, and you'll be able to raise the empathic quality of any conversation to an appropriate level. What do I mean by "appropriate"? That's another question we'll deal with in the next chapter along with some other notable considerations.

In the meantime, try your empathic skill at every opportunity in your contacts with others. Remember, the only way you can get to Carnegie Hall is to practice.

*A pigeon came home very late for dinner
one evening, with his feathers bedraggled
and his eyes bloodshot. "I was out minding
my own business," he explained, "when
bingo! I get caught in a badminton game!"*

Bennett Cerf

15

Here You Are—
There You Go

If things have worked out as I hoped when I began this book, you and I are now at about the same place. I hope that you've been able to read out of my words what I put into them. I also hope this won't be a parting of ways for us. I know that you'll need to refer to these pages frequently if you intend to become a truly skilled listener. Nevertheless, having shed that cocoon, you should now be ready to try your wings. And a few final thoughts are necessary so that you won't get caught in a badminton game along the way.

Unlike the pigeon, you won't be minding your own business exclusively; unless you've wasted your time, you'll be very much involved in helping others tend to their own business—a reciprocal process that's a lot like a badminton game, with the shuttlecock consisting of feelings. And just as in a badminton game, you'll need to know that there are times to hold your racket poised but not swing. Like shuttlecocks, empathic responses are sometimes out of bounds. And that brings us to my closing comments.

At least two considerations should be observed in the

use of empathic response. First is the matter of economy of use.

I can't think of anything that seems—and feels— more unreal than application of empathic response when the message doesn't warrant it. I've seen this demonstrated in my workshops. When sample situations are provided to which participants are directed to respond empathically, there is much discomfort when the situations give content with no apparent emotional basis. For example, how can you genuinely respond empathically to a statement such as "I'm going fishing this weekend" or "We've certainly had a long cold spell."? Small talk deserves small talk response.

The point is that sometimes feeling-level communication is appropriate, and sometimes simply dealing with content is sufficient. But even when communications are confined to the content level, remember that listening is still important—no matter what sort of response may seem appropriate. There are times when one of the various response types discussed in chapter 12 may be a more proper choice than the empathic response. You may be called upon to interpret the speaker's words, for example, if you're an instructor and he's your student. Or you may discern that the speaker really wants your reassurance, and so a supportive response is called for. If you're an attorney, there are many occasions, especially in court, when probing questions are the proper type of response to the speaker's statements. The responses classified as advice-giving are also suitable to particular situations. But regardless of the style of response, each requires the skill of listening; so listening is a generally appropriate behavior. That observation may seem needless, but recent experience tells me that a reminder is useful.

Just now I'm supervising the field work of a group of students seeking their master's degrees in marriage and family counseling. When I last met with them to review their cases, one student told me about an acquaintance who, she reported, called her frequently to tell her about some personal problem or other. The acquaintance dwelled at length and in great detail, prefacing her oration each time with a suggestion that she would like the student's advice. But when her lengthy detailing of the problem was over, it was obvious to the student that advice wasn't really wanted and that the acquaintance had decided on a course of action independent of the student. "Am I making her dependent on me by listening to her problems?"

Here was a graduate student, you see, who had completed a number of courses (I assume) in psychological theory pertinent to counseling, yet had no idea of the power of the listening ear, no idea of the dynamics going on as she listened to her acquaintance. Well, I assured her that she wasn't doing this person a disservice, that on the contrary she was providing a very valuable and scarce commodity. With all the excellent textbooks available—including those mentioned in this book—and with all the emphasis lectures give it, I can't imagine how anyone seeking a counseling degree could get as far as field work without some introduction to the art of listening and its effects.

On the subject of listening—with the "third ear"— I must mention another bit of dialogue I heard just a few days ago. An executive was telling a friend about a certain secretary in his office who had long and shapely legs and a penchant for wearing short skirts. One day the executive's secretary buzzed the intercom and announced that Ms. Shapely Legs was waiting with some papers for him to sign. He instructed his secretary to admit Ms. S.L., signed the papers, and handed them to her. He then walked to the door of his office with her and watched her retreating back as she undulated down the hall. As he turned back toward his office, he looked down to see his secretary staring at him with an accusatory expression. "I know what you're thinking," she said, to which he quickly replied, "You're wrong!"

Now that's communication—I guess. It's a lot like listening to students of the muse arguing about what a particular classical poet really meant when he wrote a certain verse, and doing so as though each speaker were personally acquainted with him.

Regardless of the fact that listening is highly desirable, and regardless of the kind of response one makes, listening isn't listening unless there's a request for feedback —a check on the listener's perception. You already know that inferences are dangerous and, more often than not, incorrect. What I said at the beginning of this book still holds: Listening is the nicest thing that two people can do for one another. Don't forget that. Remember too that the best kind of listening is the kind which shows that you're empathic. But save that empathic response, use it only when it's appropriate. I can't tell you when that is, but you'll become expert enough to tell—with practice.

In addition to the question of appropriate use of the empathic response, the second major consideration concerns the right of each of us to remain a private person. Some things we just don't wish to share, and others have no right to ask us to share them. When using the empathic response to reach deeper feeling levels, we must be perceptive enough to know when we've invaded the speaker's privacy.

Of course the speaker may simply tell you straight out that you're trespassing, but that's becoming less likely in our developing culture. We've become saturated with a seemingly endless variety of sensitivity and encounter groups. Disclosing everything about one's self has become a way of life. Not to do so is taken as an indication of defensiveness, which is "unhealthy" and an indication that the withholder is "uptight." I've personally seen the effects of some of these group experiences, and the literature on the subject is replete with case studies of individuals driven from neurosis to psychosis as a result of such experiences. Not all groups have equal potential for psychological damage, of course; but they all, perhaps, mainly benefit the completely healthy personality who doesn't need them in the first place—and as entertainment rather than therapy. For such persons are intrigued by the process, not the product, although some do get "kicks" from witnessing the personality disintegration of others.

While I think that children should begin in the early years to learn that they are feeling organisms and that they should be aware of their feelings, I don't believe that such training should turn into a wholesale onslaught against their psyches; nor do I believe that the agent for such training needs to be, or perhaps even should be, someone trained in counseling or psychology. Certain children do have behavioral difficulties which require the assistance of skilled counselors and psychologists, but not all children have such difficulties. And yet we're beginning to see total school immersion into programs aimed at the psychological development of children. The involvement of public agencies in such activities brings us dangerously close to the kind of mind control envisioned in *Brave New World* and *1984*, and some specialists are now expressing concern. One of these is sociologist Thomas J. Cottle.

As a researcher, Cottle has had to guard himself against psychologically brutalizing those from whom he's gathering information. He has often had to come to grips with the reality that he's doing more than merely gathering data, since those data represent the innermost secrets of his subjects. As Cottle puts it, "I'm often insinuating my way into the private life of someone else. 'Give me something really good.' I will think. 'Something from the deepest recesses of your soul.' "[1]

Experts also worry about the tendency in our society to bring the encounter group into the world of children. I mentioned the kinds of things being introduced into schools. As I stated, not all group experiences are harmful. Some school programs in which the group is the medium for improved social and racial relations have provided great benefits. But there is a concomitant tendency to use these groups as extensions and elaborations of the "show and tell" routine familiar to kindergarten children. This happens especially when the adult in charge fancies himself a junior grade psychotherapist and pries into the home life by urging the child to tell all.

It may startle you to learn that there are now school systems, primarily suburban middle and upper middle-class, in which participation of the children in sensitivity groups is mandatory. As early as first grade, pupils are encouraged to "get it all up front." Points are awarded for their group if they tell exactly how they feel about others no matter how much it hurts them, and they're ostracized if they don't.

Cottle mentions another interesting facet of this scholastic invasion of privacy. I'm not sure about the accuracy of his accusation that architects and school officials are conspiring to deny privacy to pupils, but there's no doubt that elimination of the individual desk and introduction of the table shared by several pupils have had that effect. Cottle also suggests that schools containing no private desks, but "open" or "cluster" arrangements of class space, are more likely to have elaborate guidance systems.[2]

Maybe much of what's happening in this "let it all hang out" fad—and let's hope it is only a fad—stems from the gradual disappearance in this country of individual responsibility. Whenever there's need for an individual to take action, some expert or specialist is always available on whom he can dump his responsibility.

When I speak to parent groups, the inevitable questions concern their child-rearing practices. When my replies are qualified by my statement that I'm only offering my own approach and that I can't and won't tell them how to raise their children, they are very disappointed. The fact is that I refuse to accept their responsibility. Instead I ask them to tell me what they're doing about raising their children, and I show them how to make it work. But that's very often too much responsibility for them to accept.

Someone who gives up individual responsibility has very little left of himself, because that act necessitates turning himself over to others completely—private thoughts and all. I hope we don't permit ourselves to become drawn into, or become a party to, such kinds of abdication.

Certainly there's benefit for the speaker when, through the process of empathy, he is permitted to examine and share his feelings of the moment. But the listener acts—or should act—as a facilitator. He does not—or should not —play the role of manipulator or trickster. Because he is genuinely interested in the speaker, he is interested in the speaker's welfare, and that means he has an obligation to restrain himself and not pry in areas where he's not welcome. Being empathic implies respect of the rights of others to their private thoughts and feelings.

And so if you've given it honest effort, you've now acquired a very powerful means of helping and of being more effective in your interpersonal relationships. I leave you now with the admonition to use your knowledge economically and perceptively. Respect your skill. Respect others. Proceed gently.

Notes

1 WHAT DO YOU MEAN, SCHIZOPHRENIC LISTENING?

Epigraph. Francis Bacon, *Essays and New Atlantis* (Roslyn, N. Y.: Walter J. Black, 1942), p. 114.

1. Muriel James and Dorothy Jongeward, *Born to Win* (Menlo Park, Cal.: Addison-Wesley, 1971), p. 45.
2. Thomas A. Harris, *I'm O.K., You're O.K.* (New York: Harper & Row, 1967).
3. S. I. Hayakawa, *Language in Thought and Action* (New York: Harcourt, Brace & World, 1941), pp. 58–60, 62.
4. Ibid., pp. 19–22.
5. Martin Buber, *The Knowledge of Man,* ed. Maurice Friedman (New York: Harper & Row, 1965), pp. 2–21.
6. Ibid., p. 175.
7. Virginia Satir, *Conjoint Family Therapy* (Palo Alto: Science & Behavior Books, 1967), pp. 63–65.
8. Paul Watzlawick, *An Anthology of Human Communication* (Palo Alto: Science & Behavior Books, 1964), pp. 4, 5.
9. Ibid., pp. 5, 6.
10. Leonard Zunin and Natalie Zunin, *Contact: The First Four Minutes* (New York: Ballantine Books, 1973), pp. 9–14.

2 THE LANGUAGE OF SCHIZOPHRENIA

Epigraph. Samuel Jay Keyser, "Psychology and the Theory of Lauguage," in *Communication, Language and Meaning,* ed. George A. Miller (New York: Basic Books, 1973), p. 13.

1. R. A. Gardner and Beatrice T. Gardner, "Teaching Sign Language to a Chimpanzee," *Science* 165 (1969): 644–672.
2. J. B. Watson, *Behaviorism* (New York: W. W. Norton Co., 1924).
3. Ivan Sechenov, "Refleksy Golovnogo Mozga" (Reflexes of the Brain), in *Psychology Today,* ed. Jean Smith (Del Mar, Cal.: CRM Books, 1970), p. 221.
4. Jean Piaget, *Language and Thought of the Child* (Cleveland: World Publishing Co., 1955). (Translation of 1923 work.)
5. Paul Watzlawick, *An Anthology of Human Communication* (Palo Alto: Science & Behavior Books, 1964), p. 39.
6. Gregory Bateson et al., "Toward a Theory of Schizophrenia," *Behavioral Science* 1 (1956): 251–264.
7. Brenden A. Maher, "The Shattered Language of Schizophrenia," in *Readings in Psychology Today,* ed. Jean Smith (Del Mar, Cal.: CRM Books, 1969), pp. 377–381.
8. Brenden A. Maher, "Language and Psychopathology," in *Communication, Language and Meaning,* ed. George A. Miller (New York: Basic Books, 1973), pp. 256–267.
9. Ibid., p. 262.
10. Paul Watzlawick, *An Anthology of Human Communication* (Palo Alto: Science & Behavior Books, 1964), p. 38.

3 EXPLORING SOME DYNAMICS
OF SCHIZOPHRENIC LISTENING

Epigraph. Paul Watzlawick, *An Anthology of Human Communication* (Palo Alto: Science & Behavior Books, 1964), p. 4.
1. Thomas Hora, "Tao, Zen and Existential Psychotherapy," *Psychologia* 2 (1959): 236–242.
2. David Fowler, "Who's Behind That Mask Behind the Mask?" *Christian Science Monitor,* 31 October 1974.
3. Frederick S. Perls, *Gestalt Therapy Verbatim* (Lafayette, Cal.: Real People's Press, 1969), p. 40.
4. Carl Whitaker, *What's New in Husband-Wife Counseling,* Taped series (Chicago: Human Development Institute, 1974).

4 TO BE THAT SELF WHICH ONE TRULY IS

Epigraph. Ralph Waldo Emerson, "Divinity School Address," in *The Best of Ralph Waldo Emerson: Essays, Poems, Addresses* (Roslyn, N.Y.: Walter J. Black, 1941), p. 43.

1. Thomas Hora, "Tao, Zen and Existential Psychotherapy," *Psychologia* 2 (1959): 236–242.
2. Abraham Maslow, *Toward a Psychology of Being*, 2nd ed. (Princeton: Van Nostrand, 1968).
3. Carl Rogers, *Client Centered Therapy* (Boston: Houghton Mifflin Co., 1951).
4. Carl Rogers, *On Becoming a Person* (Boston: Houghton Mifflin Co., 1961).
5. Arthur W. Combs and Donald Snygg, *Individual Behavior: A Perceptual Approach to Behavior* (New York: Harper & Bros., 1959).
6. Taylor Caldwell, *The Listener* (New York: Doubleday & Co., 1960).
7. Sidney Jourard, *The Transparent Self* (New York: Van Nostrand Reinhold Co., 1971), p. 137.
8. Ibid., pp. 59–60.
9. Ibid., pp. 30–33.
10. Ibid., p. 139.
11. Edwin McMahon and Peter A. Campbell, *Please Touch* (Mission, Kans.: Sheed and Ward, 1969), p. 8.
12. Martin Buber, *The Knowledge of Man*, ed. Maurice Friedman (New York: Harper & Row, 1965), p. 12.
13. Sidney Jourard, *The Transparent Self* (New York: Van Nostrand Reinhold Co., 1971), pp. 162–163.
14. Martin Buber, *The Knowledge of Man*, ed. Maurice Friedman (New York: Harper & Row, 1965), pp. 27–28.

5 SUFFER THE LITTLE CHILDREN

1. Jess Lair, *I Ain't Much, Baby—But I'm All I've Got* (Greenwich, Conn.: Fawcett Crest, 1974), p. 75.
2. Frederick S. Perls, *Gestalt Therapy Verbatim* (Lafayette, Cal.: Real People's Press, 1969), pp. 45–46.
3. Jess Lair, *I Ain't Much, Baby—But I'm All I've Got* (Greenwich, Conn.: Fawcett Crest, 1974), p. 26.
4. Ibid., p. 27.
5. Nathan W. Ackerman, "The Uneasy Family," *This Week Magazine*, 26 April 1964, pp. 6–7, 16–17.
6. Richard Gehman, "One Vote for Discipline," *This Week Magazine*, 26 April 1964, p. 24.
7. Benjamin Spock, *Raising Children in a Difficult Time* (New York: W. W. Norton Co., 1974).
8. Richard Gehman, "One Vote for Discipline," *This Week Magazine*, 26 April 1964, p. 24.

9. Frederick S. Perls, *Gestalt Therapy Verbatim* (Lafayette, Cal.: Real People's Press, 1969), p. 19.
10. Rudolph Dreikurs and Vicki Soltz, *Children: The Challenge* (New York: Hawthorn Books, 1964), pp. 301–305.
11. Virginia Satir, *Conjoint Family Therapy* (Palo Alto, Cal.: Science & Behavior Books, 1967), p. 2.
12. Pamela Swift, "Keeping up with Youth," *Parade Magazine,* 17 November 1974, p. 14.

6   YOU MADE ME WHAT I AM TODAY

Epigraph. Frederick S. Perls, *Gestalt Therapy Verbatim* (Lafayette, Cal.: Real People's Press, 1969), pp. 45–46.
1. Arthur Combs and Donald Snygg, *Individual Behavior: A Perceptual Approach to Behavior* (New York: Harper and Brothers, 1949), p. 21.
2. Carl Rogers, *On Becoming a Person* (Boston: Houghton Mifflin Co., 1961), p. 283.
3. Ibid., pp. 104–105.
4. James C. Coleman, *Abnormal Psychology and Modern Life,* 3rd ed. Glenview, Ill.: Scott, Foresman & Co., 1964), p. 149.
5. *Hamlet,* act 3, sc. 1.
6. Frederick S. Perls, *Gestalt Therapy Verbatim* (Lafayette, Cal.: Real People's Press, 1969), pp. 10–11.

7   "TEACHER! TEACHER! BILLY'S DOG GOTS PUPPIES!"

1. B. F. Skinner, *Verbal Behavior* (New York: Appleton-Century-Crofts, 1957).
2. Judith Greene, *Psycholinguistics: Chomsky and Psychology* (Middlesex: Penguin Books, 1972).
3. Sandra Blakeslee, *The Sacramento Bee,* 8 April 1973.
4. Dan I. Slobin, *Psycholinguistics* (Glenview, Ill.: Scott, Foresman & Co., 1971).
5. Jean Piaget, *Judgment and Reasoning in the Child* (New York: Humanities Press, 1947); and *Language and Thought of the Child* (Cleveland: World Publishing Co., 1955).
6. Gerard Egan, *The Skilled Helper* (Monterey, Cal.: Brooks-Cole, 1975), p. 22.

8   I FEEL, THEREFORE I AM

Epigraph. William James, "What Is Emotion?" in *Readings in*

the History of Psychology, ed. Wayne Dennis (New York: Appleton-Century-Crofts, 1948), p. 294.
1. Carl Rogers, *On Becoming a Person* (Boston: Houghton Mifflin Co., 1961), pp. 65–66.
2. William James, "What Is Emotion?" in *Readings in the History of Psychology,* ed. Wayne Dennis (New York: Appleton-Century-Crofts, 1948), pp. 290–303.
3. Martin Buber, *The Knowledge of Man,* ed. Maurice Friedman (New York: Harper & Row, 1965).

9   I Love You, But Is It All Right If I Do?

Epigraph. *Hamlet,* act 1, sc. 3.
1. "Anger Creatively Used," *Venture* 3 (1975): 34, p. 4.
2. Theodore Reik, *Listening With the Third Ear* (New York: Arena Books, 1972), p. 145.
3. Eric Berne, *Transactional Analysis* (New York: Grove Press, 1961), pp. 54–55.
4. William C. Schutz, *Joy: Expanding Human Awareness* (New York: Grove Press, 1969), pp. 27–29.
5. Bernard Gunther, *Sense Relaxation: Below Your Mind* (New York: Pocket Books, 1973), p. ix.

10   It's The Other Guy's Marble

Epigraph. Theodore Reik, *Listening with the Third Ear* (New York: Arena Books, 1972), p. 305.
1. Sidney M. Jourard, *The Transparent Self* (New York: Van Nostrand Reinhold Co., 1971), pp. 162, 163.
2. Ibid., p. 147.
3. William C. Schutz, *Here Comes Everybody* (New York: Harper & Row, 1971), pp. 281–282.
4. *Hamlet,* act 1, sc. 3.
5. Frederick S. Perls, *Gestalt Therapy Verbatim* (Lafayette, Cal.: Real People's Press, 1969), pp. 92, 99.

11   Don't Just Stand There—Listen!

1. Carl Rogers, *Client Centered Therapy* (Boston: Haughton Mifflin Co., 1951), pp. 244–247.
2. Gerard Egan, *The Skilled Helper* (Monterey, Cal.: Brooks-Cole, 1975), p. 61.
3. Paul Ekman, "Face Muscles Talk Every Language," *Psychology Today,* September 1975, pp. 35–39.

4. Brian Weiss, "The Invisible Smile," *Psychology Today,* September 1975, p. 38.
5. Chuang Tzu, *Basic Writings,* trans. Burton Watson (New York: Columbia University Press, 1964), p. 66.

12   NEITHER BURROWERS NOR LANDERS BE

Epigraph. Alexander Pope, in *A Dictionary of Thoughts,* compiled by Tryon Edwards (Detroit, Mich.: F. B. Dickerson Co., 1904), p. 634.
1. Gerard Egan, *The Skilled Helper* (Monterey, Cal.: Brooks-Cole, 1975), p. 56.
2. Elias H. Porter, *An Introduction to Therapeutic Counseling* (Boston: Houghton Mifflin Co., 1950), pp. 70–71.

13   THE RESPONSE-ABILITY IS ALL YOURS

Epigraph. Lewis Carroll. *Through The Looking Glass* (Great Britain: John C. Winston Co., 1923), p. 286.
1. Gerard Egan, *The Skilled Helper* (Monterey, Cal.: Brooks-Cole, 1975), p. 22.

14   A LITTLE LILY-GILDING: TOTAL LISTENING

Epigraph. Thomas L. Martin, Jr., *Malice in Blunderland* (New York: McGraw-Hill, 1973), p. 20.
1. Robert Carkhuff and Bernard G. Berenson, *Beyond Counseling and Therapy* (Buffalo, N.Y.: Holt, Rinehart and Winston, 1968), pp. 26–27.
2. Gerard Egan, *The Skilled Helper* (Monterey, Cal.: Brooks-Cole, 1975), pp. 59–60.
3. Donald A. Tubesing and Nancy Tubesing, *Tune In, Empathy Training Workshop* (Milwaukee, Wis.: Listening Group, 1973), pp. 105–106.

15   HERE YOU ARE—THERE YOU GO

Epigraph. Bennett Cerf. *Try and Stop Me* (New York: Simon and Schuster, 1944), p. 331.
1. Thomas J. Cottle, "Let's Keep a Few Secrets: Our Soul-Baring Orgy Destroys the Private Self," *Psychology Today,* October 1975, p. 87.
2. Ibid., pp. 22–23.

Index

217